Brennan's New Orleans Cookbook

Brennan's
New Orleans Cookbook

with the Story of the Fabulous

NEW ORLEANS RESTAURANT

Told by Hermann B. Deutsch

Edited and Illustrated

by

Deirdre Stanforth

PELICAN PUBLISHING COMPANY

Gretna 1990

Originally published by Robert L. Crager & Co., 1961
Thirteen printings

Publishing rights assigned by Robert L. Crager & Co.
to Pelican Publishing Company, 1982

First Pelican printing, 1982
Second Pelican printing, 1986
Third Pelican printing, 1990

Library of Congress Cataloging-in-Publication Data

Deutsch, Hermann B. (Hermann Bacher) 1889-
  Brennan's New Orleans cookbook : with the story of the fabulous
New Orleans restaurant / told by Hermann B. Deutsch : edited and
illustrated by Deirdre Stanforth.
      p.   cm.
  Reprint. Originally published: New Orleans : R.L. Crager, 1961
  ISBN 0-88289-382-3
  1. Cookery, American—Louisiana style. 2. Brennan's (Restaurant :
New Orleans, La.)—History. I. Stanforth, Deirdre. II. Title.
  TX715.2.L68D48   1990
  641.59763—dc20
                                                            90-30076
                                                                CIP

Manufactured in the United States of America
Published by Pelican Publishing Company, Inc.
1101 Monroe Street, Gretna, Louisiana 70053

CONTENTS

🦂

Hors D'Oeuvres

Soups

Seafood

Fowl

Meat

Game

Rice Dishes

Vegetables

Sauces

Salads

Desserts

Specialties

Drinks

New Recipes

Photographs follow page 20

The Brennan Story

The Brennans

In the wake of a dreadful potato famine during the mid-nineteenth century, a tide of immigrants swept from Ireland to the United States. They landed at four major ports of entry: New York, New Orleans, Baltimore and Boston. For the most part they settled there, keeping clannishly to themselves.

One of the principal gathering places in the New Orleans faubourg in which they established themselves was Noud's Ocean House saloon, hard by a navigation beacon on the levee. Quite naturally, thereafter, the Mississippi River pilots dubbed this light "The Irish Channel beacon." The area it marked is known as the Irish Channel to this day.

Here were born the Brennans who gave the nation one of its best known French restaurants in the heart of New Orleans' Vieux Carré. What follows is the story of that enterprise.

The first Owen Brennan came to New Orleans in the 1840's, some five or six years after an immigrant from Marseilles had arrived to found Antoine's restaurant which, like Brennan's, has been a family institution from the outset. In fact, writing in the *Saturday Evening Post,* James A. Maxwell described the Brennans as "having a tribal bond that would have abashed the Medicis."

On reaching New Orleans, the first Owen headed like a homing pigeon to the Irish Channel. There his son, another Owen, grew up to become engineer of the first sugar refinery to convert from mule power to steam. His son—Owen Patrick—was to have studied engineering not as his father had learned it, but in a college. However, he had met Ella Valentine at a dance.

He and his Nell were married and set up housekeeping in a tiny rented cottage. She was a wonderful manager and made herself an adequate—later a superlative—cook by learning all she could from a married sister, and even more from the Channel's neighborly housewives in sociable back fence conferences, especially on a washday, while the water in galvanized tubs came slowly to a boil over clay-bucket charcoal furnaces.

On April 5, 1910, their first child, Owen Edward, was born. Working all night at the foundry where he had secured his first job, the father did not learn of his son's advent until he came home at breakfast time. Almost on the instant, in the midst of his joyous awareness of fulfillment, he paused to apply for enrollment in correspondence courses in draftsmanship, metal working, and the like, resolved that his son's sire should not remain a foundry laborer.

Promotions followed one another as his natural aptitude for engineering was enriched by education; he was efficiency engineer of a great ironworks and dockyard when physicians insisted that he retire. Meanwhile the family circle had grown. Owen Edward was followed by cream skinned, titian haired Adelaide, black-haired John, Ella (who ultimately became the pillar of Brennan's), Dick—another Brennan mainstay—and Dottie.

As the family and its fortunes both increased, they moved to a series of ever more commodious houses. It remained for Owen Edward, the first-born, to renew the cycle by establishing his first independent household in the three-room half of a double-barreled shotgun cottage. This is a disappearing New Orleans survival of the pre-motor, pre-exurban era; a single story structure consisting of two parallel files of rooms, each without a hallway, every room opening directly into the one behind it.

His father had decided that Owen Edward should go to college, but "like father, like son." While still in his teens, young Owen had met 17-year-old Maud Siener at a dance, and they were married two years later, after Owen had compromised the higher education issue by studying accountancy and kindred courses at a business college. He was bookkeeper for a candy company when he and his bride moved into the shotgun cottage, and Owen set out to make his fortune as swiftly as might be, with his eye on a future that included a house like the one in which his parents assembled all the children and their in-laws for a noonday family feast each Sunday.

But Owen's establishment was launched on what proved to be the eve of a great depression in the early 1930's. Within a year the candy company began to retrench by dropping a number of its employes, Owen among them, from the payroll. Month after weary month he sought steady work, but employment was that dark and doubting era's very scarcest scarcity item. Even when he did find a place it was merely temporary, for most firms engaged workers only when they could not do without additional help, and dismissed them the moment their services could be dispensed with.

Yet Owen turned his hand to whatever offered. Pride in his ability to support his family without asking help of either his parents or Maud's—she carefully concealed the fact that her mother was secretly helping out with the rent—became a still fiercer determination when Maud became pregnant. He was finally driven to putting out punch boards on commission in neighborhood groceries, confectioneries and drugstores, though he bitterly resented work whose legitimacy was open to challenge. He was chafed almost as gallingly by a political job a friend secured for him as a cotton weigher at the public warehouse operated by the port authority, but clung to it grimly none the less. The pay enabled him to settle every bill for Maud's confinement when Owen Edward, Jr., was born, a sturdy boy, but so small at birth that the nurses nicknamed him Peewee. Somehow this was shortened to Pip, and it is as Pip that he too is now a mainstay of Brennan's, and the father of Owen Edward III.

(5)

More than ever the second Owen was thereafter determined to find for himself a place with a future offering assurance of permanent affiliation. He entered a partnership for the operation of a drugstore, the sort of establishment where pills were still rolled and capsules filled by hand. But the tensions between Owen, who used the winsome approach to bring in new customers, and the staid elder partner who felt that what had been good enough in the past should be good enough for the future, doomed this venture.

However, Owen emerged from it with enough money to buy an interest in a filling station. As before, he did his best to capitalize on the personality that was winning him an ever widening circle of friends, but in the end he came home to Maud one night and blurted out that "there just isn't enough in this oil station for two people; not when one of them has a child and a half."

Maudie loyally agreed that under the circumstances his best course was to sell his interest in the station, and bide his time until something with definite promise could be secured. During the ensuing months they pinched every penny, gave up anything that entailed expenditure beyond absolutely essential outlays, and waited.

Meanwhile Owen's brothers and sisters were going out into the world. Adelaide was graduated from high school and took a business course. One of Owen's friends found a place for her in the office he and another young lawyer shared with a brilliant business counselor, accountant and tax expert, Ralph Alexis. Ever since the visit of Russia's Grand Duke Alexis to New Orleans in 1872 inspired the selection of a mythical monarch, Rex, to rule over a one-day kingdom on Mardi Gras, every Orleanian whose first or last name happened to be Alexis almost automatically acquires the nickname of "Duke." Thus it was by this title that Owen ever afterward addressed the friend who was to play so signal a role in organizing the various Brennan enterprises.

John was a student at Louisiana State University, and cut a very handsome figure in his ROTC uniform whose boots his doting sister Ella was proud to polish when he came home from

Baton Rouge at week ends. By the time Ella became a high school sophomore, Adelaide virtually adopted her, even buying her clothes; and when Dick and Dottie were old enough for school, both Ella and Adelaide took it upon themselves to keep the two youngest siblings in pocket money.

Very abruptly the hard times and the penny-pinching Owen and Maudie were undergoing came to an end. The regional sales manager of a great distillery, who had met Owen during the latter's drugstore days when "prescription whisky" was a major item of pharmaceutical merchandise, and who had been impressed by his genial personality, offered him a position with salary and commissions as city salesman. From the first, Owen did well in this new line of endeavor. He was a born salesman.

Moreover one of his friends had taken over the Court of the Two Sisters (an old building with the largest courtyard in the Vieux Carré) and converted it into an immensely popular night club. At the very peak of success he was called up for military service, and asked Owen to manage the place during his absence. Since this could be done at night, he would be free to retain his salesman's portfolio during the day, an arrangement which would provide him with two good salaries instead of one.

In a free-spending era of wartime high pay, the profits of the Court of the Two Sisters soared to fantastic heights. Inevitably it occurred to Owen that, "if I can make a fortune for someone else at this, why can't I make one for the Brennans?" So with an enormous surplus in the bank, he turned the Court back to the wife of its absent owner, assuring her it would coast along on momentum if she did no more than keep an eye on things, and hired a reasonably honest manager to assist her.

But his search for such an establishment of his own hung fire until the night he encountered John Marchese, proprietor of a club domiciled in the Old Absinthe House. Together they turned in at a Bourbon Street bistro for a drink and in the course of casual small talk, Marchese put into words his desire to rid himself of his business. Before they parted, Owen had secured a commitment from him to hold open until the following noon a definite offer to sell the place. Returning to his home at 4 that morning, he woke Maud and said:

"Good news Blondie. The best! I just bought the Absinthe House. Not the building, of course, but the business. Johnny Marchese . . ."

"Are you out of your mind?" demanded Maud, interrupting as she came wide awake. "Where do you think you can get that kind of money?"

"We've got three thousand saved up from commissions and salaries, and I can borrow the rest from Ben and John Latino; you know, the wholesale liquor dealers. They already agreed to lend me enough, just on my note."

"And what happens if you're called up in the draft? What do I do about your note?"

"You'll hire somebody to run the place for you. Besides, with my eyes and my asthma and our kids I don't think they'd ever take me, anyway. Still and all, even if they do, you'll have something now to keep you going without having to say to your dad or mine that I went in the army without leaving you a copper cent to live on, so won't they please take you in off the street till I get back."

They talked till daylight, and gradually Maudie came around to her husband's way of thinking. By mid-forenoon she and Owen together went downtown to close the transaction since, under Louisiana law, anything acquired after marriage by either spouse becomes community property.

Jubilantly irrepressible, Owen broke the news to his parents the following Sunday at the regular family dinner.

"Mom," he announced with an impish grin, "Maudie and I have bought a saloon!"

The Old Absinthe House

The "saloon," as Owen jestingly referred to it in announcing his purchase to the family, has long been the subject of some of New Orleans' most charming—and most preposterous—legends. No one today can say just how this came about. Quite possibly Lafcadio Hearn, who supposedly was the author of a New Orleans guide book issued in 1882 for the Cotton Centennial Exposition of that year, deliberately endowed the building with fictitious glamor.

Certainly the place, now magnificently restored, lent itself readily to tall tales of a swashbuckling past. Between the second and third floors of the original building a split-level chamber for which no one ever found valid rhyme or reason, became the "secret room" in which Andrew Jackson met Jean Lafitte to enlist the latter's aid in repulsing the British invasion at Chalmette in January, 1815.

There was literally no end to myths coupling the old house with Lafitte's band of outlaws, who were romantically portrayed as pirates, smugglers, or both, at various stages in the development of New Orleans' folklore. Yet official records of the parish mortgage office reveal that the place did not become a public house of any sort until some time in the latter 1860's. Originally it was a prosaic combination of residence and store. Francisco Juncadello, a Spanish immigrant, used it as his home and as a business establishment where he dealt in imported leather goods. It is still owned by his descendants and those of his partner, Pedro Font, all of whom now reside in Spain.

However, after it became a public house, its career was undeniably checkered. As a restaurant, its corner room was set aside for dispensing absinthe, with Cayetano Ferrer, presiding genius of the French Opera House's refectory, as dispenser-in-chief. The marble bar on which absinthe was dripped became deeply pocked by the constant dropping of water from spigots mounted on low pedestals. Even after absinthe was outlawed on both sides of the Atlantic, the corner room continued to attract brisk tourist patronage.

Among the many who, at one time or another, exploited this aura of tradition were the two brothers Cazenave, Arnaud and Jules. The former, better known as "the Count" (a title he declared he could validate by returning to France) founded the restaurant which still bears his name. The latter, a scholarly graduate of the Sorbonne, took over the Old Absinthe House. Naturally enough, the blight of national prohibition threatened the success of both ventures.

Arnaud's managed to survive. The Absinthe House, in whose scheme of things food played a negligible role, might likewise have weathered the drought had not a cadre of dry raiders burst into the place one night, shattering a door Jules had purchased from the demolition of the old Hotel Saint Louis, where it had once swung wide to admit a king. The agents also played hob with the visitors' book in which generations of celebrities had inscribed their names and appropriate epigrams . . . and they finally found, and seized for evidence, exactly one-eighth of an ounce of absinthe.

Thereafter the place deteriorated. Jules abandoned it to acquire a restaurant near Lake Pontchartrain, the Moulin Rouge. The pitted marble bar was sold, its purchaser adopting for his establishment the name of "The Old Absinthe House Bar." Then Mary Lee Kelly came back from Panama.

A buxom singer from the Midwest, she had been stranded in New Orleans, where she was reduced to selling stockings at a local department store, until a Panamanian impresario engaged her to join a quartet of plump girl singers, billing them as "A Thousand Pounds of Melody" for an engagement in the Canal Zone. That launched Mary Lee on a new and spectacularly successful career as a night club operator, her establishment in the Zone being known throughout the seven seas as "Kelly's Ritz." Returning to New Orleans, the scene of her one defeat, she leased what was left of the Old Absinthe House, and gave it the garish decor so popular in the Teeming Twenties. She also added entertainers, an emcee, and a bouncer, along with guest stars, like her friend Evelyn Nesbitt Thaw, in an array that catapulted the place to brief renown.

For no discoverable reason, its popularity soon flickered out. Once more the Old Absinthe House, with its cobwebbed corners, its crumbling mortar, and its melange of fable-and-fact traditions, was given over to ever increasing dilapidation. Several subsequent efforts to rekindle the spark of gaiety there met with failure. Finally John Marchese sold the business to Owen Brennan, who installed a new bar, junked the garish furnishings, and with a great tilted mirror behind a piano in a small inner room, created an illusion of spaciousness without destroying the charm of intimacy.

He and the Roosevelt Hotel's resplendent Blue Room were the first to bring "name" night club acts to New Orleans. Ethel Waters was the initial such performer to appear at the Absinthe House. Later, when one Lucian Cazabonne discharged his pianist, the renowned Walter "Fats" Pichon, Owen immediately placed him under contract.

Each night he brought home the bankable portion of the evening's receipts, carrying the money in a cigar box which he turned over to Maudie, who was to deposit its trove of coin and currency when the banks opened later that morning. It goes without saying that no fiscal arrangement of this sort could be maintained. Though Maudie struggled courageously with it for a time, she finally rebelled, delivering a domestic ultimatum to the general effect that she was no longer going to rise at 1 or 2 o'clock in the morning, put in the remaining hours of darkness counting the money in Owen's cigar box, make out deposit slips, prepare breakfast for him and then for the children, put the house in order and at length go to the bank with hundreds of dollars in a box of which she was certain one day to be robbed.

Not only that, but Owen was finally called up for the draft. As expected, an asthmatic allergy kept him from induction; but he was instructed to find employment forthwith in some vital war industry, and so became an expediter at the Higgins plant, which at that time was turning out landing craft for the invasion forces. He worked there from 8 in the morning until 4, went home for a few hours' sleep, then stayed at the Absinthe House till closing time, snatching another brief interval of sleep till he had to set out for the Higgins plant. Obviously this left him no time for the administrative details of his night club. In this dilemma he called on his old friend, business counselor Ralph Alexis, for advice.

"I'm up against it, Duke," he declared. "In the first place, the books never balance any more, and I don't know what I'm making money on. Right now I might be making more on a plain shot of bourbon and water than I make on a Pirate's Dream."

This last was Owen's imaginative contribution to the roster of New Orleans potabilia. Served in a mammoth container not quite large enough for a sitz-bath, it was a blend of orange juice, lemon juice, two or three different kinds of rum, grenadine, some slices of assorted citrus fruits, cherries and other random ingredients. It bristled with straws like an irascible porcupine. As an item of Bourbon Street's Bacchic curiosa it still enjoys an immense vogue.

Alexis worked out a cost-accounting system and suggested putting Adelaide in charge. Owen balked at this because he did not like the idea of his sister working in what was after all a sort of glorified barroom. But he solved the dilemma by confining her hours strictly to the daytime, and by engaging Ella, newly graduated from high school, to keep Adelaide from being the only girl in the establishment. Aside from that, Ella's duties were not too clearly defined.

Next, in order to keep his young sisters away from the bar, he provided a special office for them; a third floor apartment that also did duty as a storeroom. Ella, incidentally, was forever locking her key inside this "office." Consequently, she hid a hammer and screw driver in one of the recesses of an old wall of soft rose brick. Attaining perfection through practice, she soon was adept at lifting the locked door off its hinges when she needed to gain entry and Adelaide was not there to admit her. Before long, she became a sort of general maintenance superintendent, whose competence was beyond challenge. Adelaide kept the books, paid bills and served as comptroller-in-chief.

In this revival, the fame of the Old Absinthe House spread rapidly. Nationally syndicated columnists like Earl Wilson would drop in and succumb instantly to the combination of Owen's personality, Fats Pichon's piano playing, and in all likelihood the more fissionable elements of a Pirate's Dream. Robert Ruark, a naval officer at the time, would make it a Bourbon Street port of call at every New Orleans landfall. When restored to civilian status and wide journalistic renown, he became so attached to Owen and all his tribe, that the syndicate heads who distributed his column developed a stock answer to his frequent suggestions that he leave New York periodically in quest of fresh material. It was:

"Okay, but not New Orleans again."

Hollywood celebrities made the Absinthe House a must during New Orleans visits; other tourists, to say nothing of Orleanians, were drawn by the prospect of seeing and perhaps rubbing elbows with these archangels of the entertainment skies. In short, business literally boomed; not only was the first note paid off promptly, but when Adelaide struck a balance at year's end there was more money left than any one wanted to leave idle as a cash bank deposit. This led indirectly to the birth of one of New Orleans' youngest yet most widely known restaurants which, having begun life as the Vieux Carré, in time became simply "Brennan's."

♉

"The Vieux Carré"

While it has no association, romantic or otherwise, with pirates, presidents or other personalities, the Bourbon Street building which housed the first Brennan restaurant is one of the oldest still standing within what was the original walled city laid out when Bienville founded it in 1718. It has no name. Neither the New Orleans City Guide prepared under the direction of Lyle Saxon, nor the meticulously researched history of most of the Quarter's buildings compiled by Stanley Clisby Arthur thought it worthwhile to include this structure in their roster of interesting survivals from the colonial era.

But it was almost certainly built prior to 1803, for it passed into the possession of the Widow Lieutaud in 1808, and was not new nor apparently even recent then. Its next owner of record was Mme. Elizabeth Blanc, who passed it on to her widowed daughter, Mme. Elizabeth Rea, and the latter's two children in 1841. It remained in the possession of the Rea family until 1892, when it was acquired by a Dr. Joseph Bauer, who sold it in 1919 to Justin Lacoste.

Some time during the middle 1920's Mr. Lacoste leased it to Maurice Amavet, who opened a restaurant there. A one time migrant from the south of France, Maurice was born with a genius for fine food. He developed this by working at Antoine's for 14 years as a waiter before leasing and remodeling the Lacoste building. He gave the front room a white tile floor like Antoine's, separated his kitchen from the dining room merely by swinging doors, and finally had a manufacturer of electric signs identify the premises as the Vieux Carré Restaurant. This might well have become a permanent feature of New Orleans' old quarter, had not prohibition reared its horrible head.

Maurice could no more imagine cooking or dining without wine than he could imagine breathing without air; nor did he see harm in serving well known clients some reasonably authentic Bordeaux or Burgundy, to be imbibed from thick porcelain or stoneware teacups. *Malheureusement,* two guests who dined at the restaurant regularly and long enough to win his confidence turned out to be prohibition agents, and Maurice barely escaped having his Vieux Carré summarily padlocked.

The second time this occurred, however, the padlock was imposed. Thereupon, consigning *a l'enfer* the whole madness which branded the serving and drinking of wine as both sinful and illicit, Maurice returned to Marseilles where he became in time a prosperous and successful food broker, full of years and the warm glow that follows the ingestion of fine food to the accompaniment of sound wine.

Other intermittent efforts to operate the Vieux Carré as a restaurant failed to come off during the era immediately following the withdrawal of Maurice's guidance. It was still struggling along in 1944, barely not failing, under the management of Leon Touzet, son-in-law of the Justin Lacoste who held title to the property, and through M. Touzet Owen acquired the first Brennan's.

Most of the stories of how this came about, and their number is legion, are apocryphal. Owen did nothing to contradict them, and may well have encouraged the invention of several. It is said, for example, that having lunched there one day, he harangued the proprietor for not providing better food and service, whereupon the latter retorted with some heat: "If you think you can run this place better than I do, why don't you buy it?" to which Owen replied: "Okay. How much do you want for the lease, fixtures, good will and all?"

According to another account, Owen was lunching at Arnaud's with his good friend, the Count, whose restaurant was a swiftly expanding success. The Count is alleged to have twitted Owen by saying that no Irishman could ever possess or display greater skill in matters of the cuisine than might be required to boil potatoes, to which Owen is said to have replied: "Is that so? Well, I'll just show you and the world that this Irishman can run the finest French restaurant in New Orleans, present company not excepted."

There is, to be sure, a grain of truth in all such legends. Owen and the Count did badger one another unmercifully, though always in the best of good humor. That was a matter of common knowledge. Yet the circumstances leading to the acquisition of the Vieux Carré as a Brennan enterprise were most casual. Owen and Maud were driving toward the business district on Orleans Street one morning, when they saw Leon Touzet at an intersection, waiting for a bus. Naturally, they invited him to ride with them. En route, the talk turned to the wartime difficulties of conducting any sort of business with the kind of labor available to civilian employers. Touzet seemed glad of the opportunitiy to unburden himself about a sad state of affairs in which it was all but impossible to secure competent kitchen help or waiters.

Owen said something to the general effect that the place had never been a success after Maurice Amavet's departure, and asked whether the present operators had ever considered selling out. "We've practically decided to do just that," Touzet informed him.

Before the week was out, Owen had leased the establishment. Part of the capital was furnished by his father, and a minor interest by one Louis Pallud, who had been in charge of the lunch and catering service of a large department store. Owen financed the balance. The transaction was consummated just as the elder Brennan, having recovered his health, began to rebel against retirement and a future of doing nothing but putter around the house and garden. Thus the restaurant began as a family partnership. It has remained one.

The place still bore the name Maurice Amavet had conferred upon it some twenty years earlier: The Vieux Carré. Inasmuch as this had become part of the New Orleans tradition, the sign was not disturbed; but above it another sign was installed so that the restaurant an Irish clan had dedicated to the *haute cuisine* of France as modified by Louisiana's Creoles, became "Brennan's Vieux Carré."

Major changes were wrought in the dining room at once. At Owen's insistence, the hexagonal white floor tiles were covered with a deep-piled red carpet. At Maud's suggestion, candlelight was substituted for the stark glare of incandescent bulbs. Within a year or so, Louis Pallud launched a catering establishment in another city, thus leaving Owen P. and Owen E. as sole partners.

Among the restaurant's regular noonday patrons, however, were John, Ella and Adelaide, all employed at the Absinthe House directly across Bourbon Street from the Vieux Carré, and they derived a keen satisfaction from being just as critical of the food and the service as though their sire and their elder brother were not the proprietors. Then, in a time of crisis, when a cashier left just before Christmas, Ella was called upon to take over the job. Her desk was placed so that she was able to observe everything that went on. She was thus in a position to form a shrewd estimate of just who was responsible for what mishaps. She tried to tell Owen about these.

"Not only that," she added, "but all you're doing is to give the people Trout Amandine, Oysters Rockefeller, and things like that, every one of which is identified with some other restaurant. Why not figure out something that stands for Brennan's, and make it better than any other restaurant in the whole world could make it?"

"Tell you what I'll do instead," countered Owen. "You and John have been griping about the way the place is run. So you two come over and run it. Dad will still be in charge, but you two will be doing the actual production work for the whole operation."

So Ella, all of 18 years old, and not long out of high school where she had not taken so much as a single elementary Home Ec course, was cashier. John, an experienced PBY pilot with a distinguished record of patrol bombing which had done nothing to prepare him for restaurant management, buckled down to the task in hand. He went to the local GHQ of Swift & Co., with the following request: "I don't know the first thing about meat, especially about buying it for a restaurant, so please teach me." As for Adelaide, she merely expanded her accounting practice to become comptroller-in-chief for both establishments.

Ella worked with the waiters, coaxing them into personal pride in their association with Brennan's and occasionally blazing out at them like a small teenage fury when her temper got the best of her, but always bearing in mind what Owen had once said about such eruptions: "If you're all that mad, go home and sleep on it. If you're still all that mad tomorrow we'll do something about it. But likely you won't be all that mad by then."

John did the day's purchasing early in the mornings, and then went to the floor—the dining room, that is—at lunch time, remaining there till his father came in to take over for the night. But John was in the thrall of a great desire to head his own enterprise, as well as his own dynasty. He had married nearly two years before and was the father of a son.

"You don't really need me," he told Owen. "The place is full of Brennans as it is, and when Dick and Pip finish college, there'll be still more of them. My own son, if he wants to do it when he grows up, can come over here. But I want to be on my own."

Owen agreed. "It's a good thing there's enough of us Brennans to go 'round," he grinned. "Don't forget that Pip's got two brothers coming along." Then he called in Ella and told her John was no longer in charge, having decided to strike out for himself.

"You're the general manager now, with only Dad as boss," he added. "I'll be the front man a good part of the time, but I'm not about to go near the kitchen. That will be strictly your little red wagon, as of right now."

"You mean I can do what I want about how the kitchen is

(19)

run? I can even get a little service bar back there? I can hire and fire, if I feel there's no other way to get things going the way they should?"

"I told you, kid. You're in charge out there."

"In that case I'm going right out to hire us a new chef."

Ella had tried manfully to institute changes in the kitchen's long established routine; but the old chef was set in his ways, and would brook no interference in these by any one, let alone a mere chit of a girl. He concerned himself, as always, primarily with the preparation of food in quantity, rather than with individually enticing dishes. Ella had often sought to convince him that this was not the approach Brennan's restaurant envisioned; time and again she had repeated what she once told Owen about the creation of specialties which would be identified with Brennan's. But the chef had remained obdurate. So 18-year-old Ella went back into the kitchen within moments after Owen made her the general manager, and fired him. The third cook, a studious and unassuming Hollander named Paulus Blangé, was given the title of *chef de cuisine,* and thus put in charge.

Blangé had come to New Orleans after years of experience in Dutch restaurants, in the galleys of the Holland-American line, and in those of the United Fruit Company's Caribbean fleet. One of the principal reasons for his choice by Ella was that he alone had shown real interest in her continuing demand that someone create a dish that could be identified with Brennan's as Oysters Rockefeller was with Antoine's. Paul came up with a trout item which could be prepared individually to order. This became so instantly and permanently popular that it was named for him and is served to this day as "Truite Blangé."

In New Orleans the saltwater spotted weakfish of the Gulf has been known for generations as a "speckled trout." It is the traditional component of "Truite Blangé"; but as detailed in the recipe section of this volume, any of the palatable fish varieties in which the New Orleans area abounds—redfish, red snapper, pompano, bluefish—may be used. A filet of savory fish, preferably "speckled trout," of course, is poached in a courtbouillon, covered with a

Owen E. Brennan

The Old Absinthe House before and after restoration.

thick sauce in which shrimp, oysters, crabmeat and mushrooms are bonded, and the whole is surrounded with a fluted border of duchesse potatoes.

Impressed by the popularity this specialty won so swiftly, Owen joined Ella in urging all hands to think up dishes which would be both distinctive and toothsome. He even contributed a suggestion for what is known variously as "assorted oysters," "Three Deuces," or *"Les Troix Deux."* Two of the six oysters of each portion are served with Rockefeller sauce, all six being served on the half shell, and broiled under the flame on a bed of hot rock salt, as originated for Oysters Rockefeller. The other components of this Brennan specialty are two Oysters Roffignac, and two Oysters Bienville, the three distinct and contrasting flavors serving to complement one another.

Virtually every one connected with the staff joined the drive to come up with distinctively individual items for the new Brennan specialties. Frank Bertucci, now *maitre d'hotel,* had "come with the place" as a waiter when Owen took it over. He and Andre Bitoun, another of the waiters, remembered something about a different way of making Crepes Suzette. It was vague, but they experimented and improvised and finally came up with what many connoisseurs unhesitatingly describe as the finest crepes ever confected. Many diners who have eaten elsewhere drop in at Brennan's just to enjoy these special crepes for dessert. The recipe for their preparation is also included in this book.

Finally Owen went on a still-hunt for old cookbooks, and bagged three English volumes, one of which dated back to the mid-eighteenth century. With these for a start and Ella to cheer them on, Paul and his kitchen staff each day selected a meat dish, a fish dish, and a game or poultry dish from the yellowed pages. Many of the ingredients mentioned in the curious type whose esses looked like effs were not obtainable. But pompano could be substituted for Dover sole, Four-Bayou oysters for Colchesters, and squabs for larks. Moreover, they were meticulous in observing a rule Owen had laid down at the very outset:

"No fowl of any sort is to be served at Brennan's unless it has been boned. I don't ever want to see a pretty girl in her best party frock struggle to cut shreds from a chicken, trying to appear nonchalant though she's scared to death of splashing sauce on her dress; not when we can serve fowl either in breast slices or boned, so that she can eat it with grace and dignity."

That is how *Poulet Pontalba* (see the recipe section) came into being as another favorite selection of those who dined at Brennan's during the early period of the establishment's growth, when Owen's phenomenal memory for names and faces once more stood him in excellent stead. In New Orleans almost any visiting celebrity went to Brennan's for at least one meal, knowing in advance he would be accorded the world's most genial VIP treatment. For example, Elia Kazan, long since a familiar of the Absinthe House, had not stopped over in New Orleans since the Vieux Carré passed into the possession of the Clan Brennan. But on his first visit under the establishment's new ownership he put his head in at the door one noon till his eyes met those of Owen.

"Any gumbo today?" he inquired. "And if so, how is it?"

"Come in and try," invited Owen. "We told the chef to make up a special batch every day, just on the chance you might show up."

"I'd sure like to, but I've got some one out here with me. Is it all right if I bring her along?"

The some one was Vivien Leigh. They had come to New Orleans to shoot a few scenes for *A Streetcar Named Desire,* and the director had been billboarding to his star the superlative quality of gumbo as prepared and served on its native heath. The fact that this African modification of a West Indian dish should be served in a French restaurant owned and operated by a family as Irish as Macgillicuddy's Reeks . . . well, that was New Orleans for you.

Van Heflin, still in service, came to the city unexpectedly when no hotel room was available. "No problem," Owen assured him. "Maudie and I have a couch in the living room and we'll bed you down on it for as long as you'd care to stay."

Soon thereafter, a third floor apartment opposite the storeroom-office in the Absinthe House, was equipped with a four-poster, an armoire and a bathroom. Bob Ruark was the first to make that *chambre-garnie* his New Orleans home-away-from-home.

In short, the restaurant prospered; but it did not have a really good year, financially, until 1954. It made a small profit prior to that time, and even at its worst, it had not lost more than the Absinthe House could absorb without feeling the pinch. But in the early 1950's it achieved its first major success. In great part this could be attributed to Owen's genius for publicity, as well as to the popularity of the new cuisine.

Two of Owen's inspirations for attracting public interest had their genesis during a trip he and Maudie made to Florida. In mid-journey he telephoned his sister Ella to join them, saying he wanted her to see that the world did not consist merely of the route from the Brennan home to the Brennan restaurant. One of the spots they visited was an ostrich farm whose proprietor Owen subsequently brought to New Orleans for a Sunday morning ostrich-omelet breakfast to the ladies and gentlemen of press and radio.

The meal was a genuine triumph. Naturally, no one among the guests could say with any degree of assurance whether the basic ingredients for the *pièce de résistance* had been furnished by barnyard poultry, great auks, or ostriches. But the meal was palatable and merry, there were blown ostrich eggs for the guests to take home to their youngsters—and there was a world of publicity about it later.

On their Florida trek the Brennans had also visited St. Augustine, where they toured museums and tasted what was reputed to be the water of Ponce de Leon's fountain of youth. Maudie and Ella were frankly bored by this, but Owen said: "If that's all it takes to attract people to a spot that can't offer them anything but sunshine and sand, just wait till I make with the real tradition and charm we have back home in New Orleans!"

The moment he returned he began the transformation of his dusty mezzanine split-level in the Absinthe House, turning it into a sort of museum and formally dubbing it "The Secret Room." At antique and book shops he picked up handbills advertising rewards for the return of runaway slaves, some authentic holographs of the colonial era, and a number of excellent old prints of New Orleans as it used to be. He also bought a fantastic triple barreled two-gauge shotgun, mounted on a tripod. A Chartres Street gunsmith had been trying vainly to sell this relic of the old market-hunting days. It had no possible connection with Lafitte or the Battle of New Orleans, but it looked impressive and ancient, so Owen bought and installed it in the center of the Secret Room's floor. Then he purchased clothing-store dummies and tricked them out in pirate costumes furnished by Mardi Gras suppliers. These he posed about the room (one of them just climbing up through a newly made trap door in the floor), and insisted thenceforth that this was the apartment where Lafitte had met General Jackson to arrange for their alliance in the Battle of New Orleans.

The Secret Room cost a great deal, and this at a time, as Ella still recalls, "when we were crying the eyes out of our heads to get the stairway at the restaurant glassed in, and the entrance moved. But Owen said those things were only physical improvements while what he was doing was promotion!"

When Lucius Beebe made one of his visits to New Orleans, Owen met the train with a horse and buggy and Papa Celestin's band, which had been brought out of retirement for the occasion. The horse and buggy notion was the best with which Owen could come up at the time, since he was lamenting the fate that had withheld from Brennan's anything like what another restaurant had just received via a current best seller, Frances Parkinson Keyes' *Dinner at Antoine's*.

"If only something like that could have happened to Brennan's," he said wistfully to Beebe as their horse clop-clopped over the paving. "As it is, we can't even follow suit. If we tried to do something about Dinner at Brennan's now it would really be a nothing."

"Why does it have to be a dinner?" asked Beebe. "Why couldn't it be breakfast? What's wrong with Breakfast at Brennan's?"

Without further ado, they collaborated on an exotic breakfast menu, one version of which was: Absinthe Suissesse, grilled grapefruit, eggs Sardou, bananas Foster and coffee, accompanied by jelly and hot French bread instead of toast. As a further step in popularizing breakfast at Brennan's, a highly stylized gamecock (morning being synonymous with a cock's crow) was selected as a permanent armorial bearing for the establishment.

So enthusiastic was public acceptance of this and other Brennan innovations that Owen began to give serious thought to expanding the enterprise. Within the circumscribed confines of the building leased from Justin Lacoste, this was impossible, since enlarged kitchen facilities, wine storage space, cloak room facilities and other collateral appointments must be supplied along with more tables and space to place them. Yet when Owen confided to the Clan what new site he had in mind as the future home for Brennan's he was greeted with a chorus of protest that ranged from mere doubt to ridicule.

"That place has been a jinx for a hundred and fifty years or more . . . nobody who ever tried to run a restaurant there came even close to succeeding . . . when I think of what it will cost to do the things you're proposing I wonder if you're in your right mind, even . . ."

One associate agreed with him from the first. This was the level-headed expert who could glance at a balance sheet and learn all he or any one else really needed to know about a venture's past record and future prospects: Ralph Alexis, "The Duke." He declared unhesitatingly that what Owen proposed was well worth looking into, and so far as jinxes went, no Brennan he had ever met seemed to be truly afraid of them. In short, he would see what could be done.

I V

𝔶

Brennan's Restaurant

For more than a century and a half the building at 417 Royal Street in New Orleans seemed to have been permanently indentured to ill fortune. *Don* Jose Faurie built it as a residence in 1801, quite possibly to designs by Benjamin Henry Bonneval Latrobe, who is known to have drawn the plans for two famous structures on either side of it. Although Latrobe did not come to New Orleans until 1818, the year of the city's first centennial, his work preceded him in several documented instances. He was commissioned by Treasury Secretary Gallatin in 1804 to design a lighthouse for the Balize at the Mississippi's mouth; in 1807 a customs house was built in New Orleans to Latrobe's plans.

An authentic genius, he is generally credited with being the father of architecture in the United States. As such, he is primarily responsible for the Greek classic revival in the design of so many of our public buildings, so that court houses, banks, city halls and the like throughout the country became minor and major imitations of the Parthenon. He likewise fell victim to one of the chain of tragedies that dogged the Faurie mansion from its beginnings.

He had built the Bank of Pennsylvania in Philadelphia, the

Cathedral in Baltimore, and the Schuylkill Waterworks; he was summoned to Washington to restore the Capitol which the British burned during the War of 1812. In 1817 he sent his son, Henry, to New Orleans to construct the waterworks he had been engaged to design there. But within the year Henry succumbed to yellow fever which, in that era, visited New Orleans annually as a summer pestilence. Bent on completing the work his son had begun, the senior Latrobe followed him to New Orleans, and himself died of yellow fever two summers later.

Faurie, first owner of the mansion, apparently met with financial reverses shortly after the house was completed, for he sold it in 1805 to the *Banque de la Louisiane* whose ornate BL monogram is still preserved in the wrought iron balcony railings of what is now Brennan's. The Bank of Louisiana sold the building to Martin Gordon who entertained Andrew Jackson as his house guest there in 1828. One may yet envision the General, in full uniform, descending the grand staircase to the carriageway with his host for an evening at the opera or some other function.

Gordon also lost his fortune, though as president, Jackson subsequently appointed him to the lucrative federal post of Collector of the Port. The house's next owner of record was Judge Alonzo Morphy, whose prodigy of a son, Paul Charles, became a chess master at 10, was ultimately recognized as the greatest chess player in the world—and died as a comparatively young man, mindless and broken in health. The Faurie mansion was known thereafter as the Morphy House, which led to a good deal of confusion, since the original Morphy House, where Paul Charles was born, stands in Chartres Street. But it was very briefly the residence of General Beauregard after the Civil War, and is therefore still called the Beauregard House.

As the Morphy House the stately mansion at 417 Royal Street ultimately fell upon evil days, but retained the name until, decades later, the Junior League opened a restaurant there and rechristened it "The Patio Royal." Title to the property was finally acquired by W. Ratcliffe Irby, a wealthy patron of the arts, who had a deep interest in preserving and restoring historically significant structures throughout the French Quarter. Thereupon the malignant fate that seemed to hover over those associated with the Faurie mansion added another chapter to its chronicle.

In 1926 Mr. Irby went to an undertaking establishment, selected a coffin, paid for it, stepped into an adjoining room and shot himself. His will deeded the Morphy House, as it was then still called, to Tulane University which later leased it to a series of occupants. One of these, a formerly very successful restaurateur, was rapidly approaching the point at which his investment would be a total loss when Owen Brennan conceived the idea that the historic building could be remodeled into a genuinely attractive restaurant. As for the bad luck that had dogged it in the past, the Clan Brennan was adept at thumbing its noses at superstitions.

From November, 1954 until May, 1955, the Brennans conferred with their architects, Richard Koch and Sam Wilson, and with the Vieux Carré Commission, a body which has the legal authority to sanction or veto proposed remodeling, razing, or other structural changes affecting any sites of historic interest or importance in the French Quarter. In this instance, no end of vexatious difficulties had to be overcome. The architects would knit their brows over the need to install a dishwashing machine or an ice maker, without destroying the original Faurie mansion's historical integrity.

"When we figured on this in advance," Owen would remind them plaintively, "you said there were more than enough square feet to do it."

True enough, he was assured, but it now seemed quite a lot of the square feet simply were not in the right places. Something would have to be done about the zoning ordinance too. If the premises should stand vacant more than six months, the permit to conduct a commercial establishment there would automatically expire. So, on November 1, 1955, Owen officially opened a small bar in what had been the Faurie carriageway. This facility grossed no more than five or six dollars a day in the early stages of its existence, and most of the money taken in represented what Owen himself had spent when bringing visitors into the place and standing treat before pointing with pride to progress in the work of renovation.

To the unschooled eye the place was still a shambles. Material was piled about the patio in jackstraw disarray; the architects and Owen's father wandered about the littered rooms with no discernible purpose other than to kick aside odds and ends of lumber; workmen scurried about in the seemingly aimless fashion that to a non-initiate spells sheer chaos. One or two old patrons dropped in, shook their heads in bewilderment as they took in the knacker's-yard of scattered materials, and drifted out. But Owen reveled in it all. The end was in sight. The jinx would be broken. When Ralph Alexis came by to see how things were going, Owen hurried to greet him.

"Duke," he enthused, "you've done a masterful job, showing us how to lick this thing, right from the beginning. And now that it's practically behind us, what'll we do for the Absinthe House?"

Two evenings later Owen, a Chevalier of the Confrerie du Tastevin, a society founded in Dijon during the sixteenth century, attended the eighth annual *chapitre* of its New Orleans commandery. This was not merely a convivial gathering for the enjoyment of superb food and wines. Four Orleanians of note were to be inducted into the organization receiving the accolade of knighthood from a century-old grape stock. They were Darwin Fenner, social, business and civic leader and partner in a far-flung national network of brokerage offices; Richard Jones, executive vice president of the Jackson Brewing Corporation, one time commodore of the Southern Yacht Club, commander of the Louisiana division of Sportsman Pilots, president of International House; George Farnsworth, head of one of the South's largest construction companies; and Joseph Montgomery, vice president of the United Fruit Company.

Neither they nor any of the other diners enjoyed the *chapitre* more whole-heartedly than Owen. He partook in moderation of the incomparable wines: Puligny Montrachet 1945, Chambertin Clos de Beze 1949, Richebourg 1948, and Chateau d'Yquem 1947.

He ate with relish of the matchless food, beamed happily upon his friends . . . in short, it was for him a wholly delightful evening, so much so that when he returned to his home he woke Maud to tell her about it.

In the morning Maud, coming to wake him, found that he had died in his sleep.

His limbs were composed, however, as in natural slumber. There had been no panic foreboding or awareness of imminent extinction, no struggle for breath. Owen Brennan had gone happily to bed. Sleep and happiness would be unbroken throughout eternity.

After the shock of Owen's passing had eased, a family council was convened to consider two questions. The first: What would Owen want us to do? The second: Can we do it without him? The reply to both—the only possible answer—was a decision to complete the work as he had envisioned it, down to and including the restoration of the Absinthe House. From November, 1955, to May 1956, therefore, all hands worked toward a common goal: the transfer of Brennan's to its future home must be made on the day Owen had planned to make it, and the new establishment must be in mint condition when its doors were opened. No one was ever to say: "We'll do better after things settle down a bit."

Ever since the Faurie-Gorden-Morphy mansion first became a public house, Patio Royal by name, a dining room had occupied the front of its street level floor, while the kitchen had been tucked away in the rear cubicles where slaves had once been quartered. The Brennan design installed the kitchen where the front dining room used to be. It also provided for the removal of partitions so that an ell-shaped area at ground level became the dining hall, from which guests could look out upon the patio through glass doors topped by beautifully fashioned fan lights. No food would be served in the patio. Its glass topped tables of wrought iron would be used by guests who desired to sip drinks while waiting for their dining room reservations.

A dull green awning which in the past had been stretched over the patio in rainy weather, and the taut wires that supported it were all abolished. The courtyard became what the long-dead architect who designed it had intended it to be: a walled-in garden whose ornamental shrubbery, clustered banana palms and towering magnolia tree starred with fragrant cream-colored blossoms in the springtime, would be screened from the gaze of passers-by in the Rue Royale. One addition to its original furnishings would be made. Clay heat reflectors would shed a warm glow on the courtyard and its galleries during occasional onsets of winter chill, so that the garden's beauty could be enjoyed the year 'round.

Owen Patrick Brennan was a veritable tower of strength during this trying period, though already past the Biblical allotment of three score years and ten. His professional knowledge of materials, his skill in translating blueprints for the workmen, and above all his serenity amid the pushes and pulls of crisis after crisis stilled any doubts that might arise as to the successful completion of the task the Clan had set for itself. As for Ella, she seemed to have become twins. One of her was apparently always on hand in the old restaurant; at the same time she seemed never absent from the new one. "Owen'll haunt you if you make us miss the opening day he set," was a threat with which she met any slowdown that might be impending.

Days and weeks sped by. A new year dawned. Carnival was climaxed by Mardi Gras, after which most of the city entered upon a season of sober austerities in Lenten self-denial. And then it was Easter Sunday on the first day of April. The rush of work at the Patio was intensified as the end of their striving drew near.

On May 31 breakfast was served at the old place opposite the Absinthe House as usual, if anything connected with a Brennan breakfast can be referred to properly as "usual." Lunch was to be served at the new restaurant; everything not indispensable to the preparation and service of breakfast had been packed and transported by professional movers the night before. Yet the venture faced an ominous drawback to its beginnings. A weeping rain had set in with the dawn, and continued to fall in a steady downpour.

None the less, as the forenoon wore to what promised to be a dreary close, more and ever more of Brennan's best known regular patrons began to drift in. Among them were merchant princes, bankers, professional men, newspaper folk, dowagers, entertainers, debutantes, and a large leaven of advertising and public relations executives.

"I thought everyone understood lunch was to be at the new place," Ella faltered, as the number of arrivals increased steadily.

"You bet we understand," she was assured. "What we're doing here is that we came to help you move!"

And that was it. An acknowledged *grande dame* took half a dozen cloths from as many tables at which breakfast had been served, a legal luminary stacked a few plates, the top copy writer for one of the city's biggest advertising agencies stuffed tableware into his pockets and then picked up a couple of chairs. Beaming, Ella called for silence.

"Everybody gets a last drink here," she announced, "and then we start. Line up at the little service bar and name your choice."

And then—Great Jelly Roll in the Morning!—just as they finished their drinks a jazz band came swinging down Bourbon Street in the rain, tearing the living tripes out of "When the Saints Go Marching In!" Carrying chairs, silverware, porcelain or whatever, they all fell in behind the musicians and marched in the rain, and with the impromptu assistance of traffic policemen in defiance of one-way arrows, down the Rue Royale to the carriageway through which General-and-President Andrew Jackson had once returned to his luxurious guest chamber. Here, there, and everywhere, the volunteers deposited their cargo.

Ella thought: "If only Owen could have seen them march behind that band!" Retiring to the wine cellar, she gave way to brief tears. Then she emerged, a charming hostess and a no less efficient executive, to preside over the first meal served at the new Brennan's. The staff had not attempted a formal, sit-down luncheon. But the buffet was magnificent, and the garniture, in which Paulus Blangé and assistants had outdone themselves, was as delightful a feast to the eye as what it garnished was to the palate

. . . and by dinnertime that evening the customary Brennan specialties were served at candle-lit, damask clad tables, while a spotlight turned into flashing crystal the falling water of a fountain that plashed before one of the old rose-brick walls of the patio. In a matter of hours, quite literally all hands had moved Brennan's to its new home.

The establishment was an immediate and runaway success, so that only one problem connected with the family enterprise remained to be solved. Its terms were implicit in the query Owen had addressed to Ralph Alexis a day or so before he died. It was: "Now what'll we do about the Absinthe House?"

This was still the most popular night spot in the Quarter. All the world had heard about the place, and while much of the report was sheer fable, even this attracted diversion seekers to the storied old bar. However, one small corner of the building was the only portion thereof which could be regarded as safely intact. The rest had been wisely shut off by reason of the physical deterioration of walls, supporting beams and roof. Only a major reconstruction project could save it. As before, the plans for achieving this had to be approved in advance by the Vieux Carré Commission. Among other things, divers additions which one occupant or another had made to the original building from time to time had to be razed. The "secret room" with its pirate clad effigies and outsize triple barreled shotgun was another and not too deeply mourned casualty. The gun is still on view behind the bar as a curio, and the effigies are placed here and there about the premises.

Nearly four years of planning and construction went into what is undoubtedly one of the finest restorations in all the Vieux Carré. It is now much in demand for background shots in television and movie productions. All in all, Owen's question about what would be done for the Absinthe House has been answered in full.

The Clan goes forward with the enterprise Owen launched. Since Brennan's became one of New Orleans' most famous dining places, Owen's parents and his close friend Ralph Alexis have joined their forebears; but other and younger members of the family are carrying on the great tradition. Among them are Owen's sons; also his younger brother, Richard. Pip—Owen Edward, Jr. —is already an assistant manager and likewise an ancestor as the father of Owen Edward III. Ella, while continuing to play a leading role in the restaurant's management, is, as Mrs. Paul A. Martin, the mother of two children. Adelaide is still standing watch with Ella at the helm. Dottie (Mrs. Bridgeman) and Barbara (Mrs. Pip Brennan) head the reservation department by day and welcome arriving patrons.

Owen will always be a living part of the establishment he did so much to bring into being. His nature included all the world in the genial warmth of its embrace.

It seemed doubly tragic that one who had faced the future with such gay confidence should have been denied the satisfaction of achievement as he stood on the very threshold of the desired goal. However, nothing can now alter the fact that in his brief, cheery life he had known no bereavement. The twinkling-eyed grin with which he had greeted each new day would never be erased by grief. Death had come very gently to a very gentle man. The foregoing narrative of his achievements is a small tribute to the lasting memory of his presence for a time among us.

Creole Cuisine

There is no such thing as "the" French cuisine. For example, the highly developed *cuisine classique,* which owes its origins to Italy, is nothing like the delightful and hearty provincial cookery of a farm kitchen in the Marne.

It is this provincial fare, and not the *haute cuisine,* from which the *Cuisine Creole* derives. "Creole" is the French for the Spanish "criollo," a term coined to designate Spaniards born in the American colonies of Spanish parentage, as distinguished from those born in the motherland and residing in America as political appointees of the Crown.

A Creole, therefore, is the descendant, born in the colonies, of French or Spanish ancestry. In Louisiana the mothers of the first Creoles were girls given a dowry by Louis XV, provided the girls, whose parents were too poor to endow them with a marriage portion, would agree to emigrate to Louisiana and, as wards of the Ursuline nuns, marry a French colonist.

These girls, reared in the provincial kitchens of their motherland, had learned how to combine a handful of herbs from hedgerow or ditchbank with an oxtail, or some frogs, snails or crayfish into the savory main dish of a satisfying meal. Frog legs *paysanne* and Chicken Marengo today class as gourmets' delights.

Bringing these skills to Louisiana they found in place of the pinched austerity with which of necessity they had to make do at home an incredibly lavish abundance. But they also found much more.

Slaves from Africa, having managed to conceal in their wool a few seeds from the *gombo* plant of their native soil, planted them in the Antilles and later in Louisiana where they flourished amazingly as okra. From Choctaw squaws they acquired *filé* powder, the dried leaves of aromatic sassafras pulverized in wooden mortars. From the Spanish they got the seeds of fiery red Cayenne peppers, and learned about rice—cheap, nourishing and growing abundantly in Louisiana.

Thus the provincial pot-au-feu of France was transmuted into Okra or *filé* gumbo, rice became the vehicle of jambalayas with the lavish abundance of seafood readily available to all, *bouillabaisse* became *courtbouillon* and crushed red peppers were metamorphosed into *sauce piquante* to ennoble otherwise commonplace fare.

Recipes for these and other Creole dishes were passed on from one generation to the next by precept and oral tradition. But within the past half century they have been collected into various compendia, each collector recording his or her particular variations on the general theme of the *cuisine Creole*. Those given herewith are the recipes which placed Brennan's at the top in the esteem of a community that prides itself on its discriminating judgment in matters of food.

They are as accurate as it is humanly possible to transcribe in specific terms what is essentially a highly individual art. Any recipe is no more than an approximation of the materials which, in skilled hands, produce excellent results, but which are invariably modified by each chef who combines them. Meanwhile, take the Clan's word for it that no "secret" ingredients have been omitted from any of the following directions. They are the very proportions used at Brennan's, as precisely and as fully as it is possible to list them.

Those who worked them out tender to all who seek to follow them their very best wishes for a triumphantly successful outcome.

Breakfast

E G G S   B E N E D I C T

🎷

2 Holland rusks
2 large thin slices ham, grilled
2 eggs, soft poached
¾ cup Hollandaise Sauce (page 190)

Cover Holland rusks with ham, then eggs, then Hollandaise sauce. Top each egg with a slice of truffle and garnish with sprig of parsley. Serve immediately. 1 serving.

EGGS BOURGUIGNONNE

❦

SAUCE

⅓ *cup finely chopped onion*
⅓ *cup finely chopped shallots*
2 tablespoons minced garlic
2 tablespoons butter
¼ *cup flour*
1 cup whole canned tomatoes
¼ *cup liquid from snails*
1 can (4½ oz.) snails
¼ *cup diced, cooked carrots*
Salt and pepper to taste
6 eggs

In a 9-inch skillet over medium heat, saute onion, shallots and garlic in butter. Stir in flour and brown thoroughly over low heat. Blend in tomatoes and liquid from snails. Add snails, carrots, salt and pepper, cook slowly 10 to 15 minutes, stirring constantly. Yield 1½ cups.

Make three 2-egg omelets and fold ¼ cup sauce into each omelet. Roll omelet onto luncheon plate and spoon sauce beside it. 3 servings.

CREAMED EGGS CHARTRES

❦

1 cup finely shredded white onions
⅓ cup butter
¼ cup flour
2 cups milk
1 egg yolk
¼ teaspoon salt
¼ teaspoon cayenne
4 hard cooked eggs, peeled and sliced,
    reserving 4 center slices for garnish
2 tablespoons Parmesan cheese
1 tablespoon paprika

In a 9-inch skillet over medium heat, saute onion in butter until transparent. Stir in flour and cook slowly 3 to 5 minutes more. Blend in milk and egg yolk until smooth. Add salt and pepper. Cook, stirring constantly, 8 to 10 minutes or until sauce thickens. Remove from heat, add sliced eggs and mix lightly. Spoon into 2 8-oz. casseroles and sprinkle lightly with paprika and Parmesan cheese mixed together. Place in oven until thoroughly heated. Garnish with egg slices. 2 servings.

EGGS HUSSARDE

❦

2 large thin slices ham, grilled
2 Holland rusks
¼ cup Marchand de Vin Sauce (page 191)
2 slices tomato, grilled
2 eggs, soft poached
¾ cup Hollandaise Sauce (page 190)

Lay a large slice ham across each rusk and cover with Marchand de Vin Sauce. Cover next with tomato and then egg. Top with Hollandaise Sauce. Garnish with sprinkling of paprika. 1 serving.

EGGS SARDOU

🌒

1 cup creamed spinach, piping hot
2 artichoke bottoms, warmed in salted water
2 eggs, poached
¾ cup Hollandaise Sauce (page 190)

Make a base of spinach on serving plate, place artichoke cups on top. Put an egg in each and top with Hollandaise sauce. 1 serving.

EGGS ST. DENIS

🌒

2 Holland rusks **
2 slices grilled ham
2 eggs, poached †
1 cup Marchand de Vin Sauce (page 191)

Put rusks on a luncheon plate. Place ham across both. While poaching, keep rolling eggs over so that whites cover whole egg and begin to puff. Place eggs over ham and top with Marchand de Vin Sauce. 1 serving.

---

* English muffins or buttered toast may be substituted for rusks if preferred.
† Poach eggs in hot lard or oil.

EGGS A LA TURK

❧

2 cups Turk Sauce
4 shirred eggs
Parsley for garnish

TURK SAUCE

¾ cup butter
½ cup coarsely chopped chicken livers
½ cup finely chopped green onions
¾ cup chopped mushrooms
¼ cup flour
¾ cup beef stock
½ teaspoon salt
½ teaspoon white pepper
½ cup red wine

In a 7-inch skillet over medium heat, saute in butter the chicken livers, green onion and mushrooms about 5 minutes. Add flour, stir constantly over low heat until flour is very brown. Blend in beef stock, salt, pepper, red wine thoroughly. Simmer 15 to 20 minutes. Yield: About 2 cups sauce.

Put 2 tablespoons of Turk Sauce in a shirred egg dish. Break 2 eggs in each dish and bake in 350° oven until eggs are firm. Cover eggs with two more tablespoons of sauce (for each dish), sprinkle with parsley, and serve.

GRILLED GRAPEFRUIT

♊

1 large grapefruit, halved
About 4 tablespoons sugar
2 oz. Kirschwasser

Prepare grapefruit by removing core and loosening meat from skin. Sprinkle top generously with sugar and then Kirschwasser. Broil for 2 to 3 minutes or until top starts to brown. Garnish with maraschino cherries and mint sprigs. 2 servings.

OMELETS

🙜

2 eggs
1 tablespoon milk or cream
¼ teaspoon salt
Dash pepper
1 tablespoon butter

Beat eggs, milk, salt and pepper together with a fork. Heat butter in 8-inch skillet or omelet skillet. Pour in egg mixture and stir. Reduce heat and cook without stirring. Lift edges from time to time to keep omelet free of pan. Slight shaking motion of skillet will tell whether or not omelet is sticking. Cook until eggs set with golden bottom and creamy top. Fold omelet and turn into heated serving dish. 1 serving.

CHICKEN LIVER OMELET

Salt and pepper 1 cup chicken livers to taste. Saute until brown and tender in butter. Remove chicken livers and add 1 teaspoon flour, stirring until brown. Add ½ cup chicken stock and livers, and simmer 10 to 15 minutes. Put one generous spoonful of this mixture inside omelet fold, pour remaining mixture over omelet. 1 serving.

SHRIMP OMELET

Saute in butter 1 cup boiled shrimp, ⅓ cup chopped shallots. Add ⅓ cup whole tomatoes. Simmer 10 minutes. Put one generous spoonful of this mixture inside omelet fold and pour remaining mixture over folded omelet. 1 serving.

SNAIL OMELET

Put one generous spoonful of Snails Bourguignonne (page 74) inside omelet fold. Add ¾ cup more over the folded omelet. 1 serving.

CRAB MEAT OMELET

Saute ⅓ cup finely chopped shallots in 1 tablespoon butter. Add ⅓ cup white crab meat and saute a few minutes. Sprinkle lightly with salt and pepper. Break eggs into pan with crab mixture to make an omelet. 1 serving.

LAMB CHOPS MIRABEAU

2 tablespoons warm tomato sauce (page 192)*
2 lamb chops, grilled rare, medium or well done
2 tablespoons Bearnaise Sauce (page 185)
3 to 4 strips crisply grilled bacon

On a dinner plate first place the tomato sauce, then lamb chops in crisscross fashion. Dot the eye of each chop with a tablespoon Bearnaise Sauce and surround the chops with bacon. Serve piping hot. 1 serving.

* Heinz tomato sauce may be used.

RIS DU VEAU LYONNAISE
(Sweetbreads Lyonnaise)

⚜

⅓ cup sliced onions
⅓ cup butter
2 tablespoons flour
1 cup milk
1 egg yolk
6 slices crisp bacon, chopped
½ cup sauterne
¼ teaspoon salt
⅛ teaspoon cayenne
6 sweetbreads, parboiled * and sliced

In a 9-inch skillet over medium heat, saute onions in butter 2 to 3 minutes. Stir in flour and cook 5 minutes more. Blend in milk, egg yolk until smooth. Add bacon, wine, salt and pepper. Continue cooking 10 to 15 minutes, stirring constantly. Add sweetbreads and heat through. Serve in 8-oz. casseroles with garnish of parsley sprig. 3 servings.

* Parboil cleaned sweetbreads in 1½ quarts water, 2 bay leaves, 1½ teaspoons salt and ⅛ teaspoon cayenne about 10 minutes, drain.

VEAL KIDNEYS FLAMBÉE

❦

SAUCE

⅓ cup finely chopped shallots
⅓ cup butter
2 tablespoons flour
1 cup milk
1 egg yolk, slightly beaten
½ cup chopped mushrooms
½ cup sauterne
¼ teaspoon salt
⅛ teaspoon cayenne

1 large veal kidney, cleaned, parboiled and
    sliced ½ inch thick
3 oz. brandy

In a 9-inch skillet over low heat, saute shallots in butter being careful not to brown. Stir in flour and cook three to five minutes more. Blend in milk and egg yolk until smooth. Add mushrooms, wine, salt and pepper. Continue cooking, stirring occasionally, 10 to 15 minutes. Yield: 2 cups.

Brown kidney slices on grill. Remove to metal serving platter, pour brandy over all and set aflame. While flaming, baste kidney slices with warm brandy. Be careful not to flame too long (about 1 minute is sufficient) or kidney will toughen.

Arrange kidney slices on plates, spoon warm brandy over top and cover with sauce. Serve remaining sauce in sauce boat. 3 servings.

Hors d'oeuvres

CANAPE LORENZO

🦂

3 tablespoons butter
¼ cup finely chopped green onion
¼ cup flour
¾ cup fish stock
3 tablespoons white wine
¼ teaspoon salt
Dash cayenne
1 egg yolk, beaten
1 cup lump crab meat
2 teaspoons chopped parsley
2 buttered toast circles, 4″ diameter
4 anchovy filets
4 teaspoons paprika
2 teaspoons buttered bread crumbs
1 teaspoon melted butter

Over medium heat in a skillet, melt butter and saute onions until tender. Blend in the flour thoroughly. Cook slowly about 5 minutes, stirring constantly, do not brown. Remove skillet from heat. Blend in fish stock, wine, salt and pepper until smooth. Blend in egg yolk thoroughly. Return pan to heat and gently cook over low heat stirring constantly about 15 minutes. Stir in crab meat and parsley, mix well. Mound this mixture high on toast circles and crisscross with the anchovies. Mix paprika and bread crumbs together and cover surface of canape. Drizzle with butter and place in preheated oven at 350° (moderate oven) for about 15 minutes. 2 servings.

SEAFOOD CANAPE

❧

1 cup chopped green onions
1 cup butter
1½ cups flour
1 quart fish stock (made from heads and bones)
1 cup white wine
4 egg yolks
1 lb. shrimp
1 dozen oysters
2 lbs. trout filets
6 Holland rusks
6 filets of anchovy
Bread crumbs
Salt, pepper and paprika

Saute green onions in butter. Stir in flour, but do not brown. Gradually add the fish stock, and white wine with egg yolks beaten into it. Season with salt and pepper. Simmer until it thickens into a heavy roux.

Boil the shrimp in their shells for 10 minutes, then peel and chop. Scald * oysters and chop. Boil trout for 5 minutes and cut it up. Add trout, shrimp, and oysters to roux, mix in and remove from heat. Let cool for ease of handling. Make a mound of this on each Holland rusk. Garnish each with 1 filet of anchovy, paprika and bread crumbs, dot with butter and bake in 350° oven 5 minutes, and serve. Serves 6.

* Put oysters in water. Bring water to a boil, and remove oysters at once.

COQUILLE ST. JACQUES

¼ *lb. butter*
¾ *cup chopped green onions*
4 tablespoons flour
2 cups fish stock
½ *cup white wine*
½ *cup cooked mushrooms*
2 egg yolks
3 cups cubed boiled fish
2 tablespoons Parmesan cheese
1 tablespoon paprika
Mashed potatoes
Salt and pepper

Saute onions in butter, add flour and mix well. Gradually stir in fish stock and wine. Add mushrooms and egg yolks, well beaten with 2 tablespoons fish stock or wine (to insure smooth mixing). Add fish. Fill coquille shells, and garnish with border of potatoes. Sprinkle with cheese and paprika mixed, dot with butter, and bake at 350° until browned (5–10 minutes). 4 servings.

CRAB MEAT CREPES

❧

3 tablespoons butter
¼ cup finely chopped green onions
¼ cup flour
¾ cup fish stock
¼ cup white wine
¼ teaspoon salt
Dash cayenne
1 egg yolk, beaten
1 cup lump crab meat

In 9-inch skillet over medium heat, melt butter and saute onions until tender. Blend in the flour thoroughly. Cook slowly about five minutes, stirring constantly. Do not brown. Remove from heat. Blend in fish stock, wine, salt and pepper until smooth. Blend in egg yolk thoroughly. Stir in crab meat and return pan to heat. Gently cook over low heat, stirring constantly about 15 minutes. Sauce will be thick.

See Crepes Suzette recipe to make pancakes. Roll each cake with 3 tablespoons of crab meat mixture. Pour remaining mixture on either side of the cakes. Garnish with chopped parsley. 4 servings.

CRAB MEAT RAVIGOTTE

❧

1 cup mayonnaise
2 tablespoons minced parsley
2 tablespoons capers, finely chopped
1 tablespoon dry mustard
1 tablespoon horseradish
2 tablespoons chopped pimiento
1 hard cooked egg, finely chopped
½ teaspoon lemon juice
2 cups lump crab meat

Thoroughly mix first 8 ingredients. Add crab meat and toss lightly; chill. Heap into shell or ramekin for individual serving. Garnish with crisscross of 2 slices of pimiento and half-slices tomato. 4 servings.

CRAB MEAT TIMBALE

❧

1 chopped pimento
4 chopped anchovies
½ cup mayonnaise
3 tbsps unflavored gelatin
1 cup vinegar
½ tsp pepper
½ tsp salt
1 can crab meat

Dissolve vinegar and gelatin in cup. In a bowl, mix together mayonnaise, chopped pimentos and anchovies. Season with salt and pepper. Add crab meat; then add the mixture of vinegar and gelatin with ingredients in bowl. Mix well. Put in cup or mold. Refrigerate for 1 hour.

OYSTERS BIENVILLE

🦪

3 tablespoons butter
¼ cup finely chopped green onions
¼ cup flour
¾ cup fish stock
3 tablespoons white wine
¼ teaspoon salt
Dash cayenne
1 egg yolk, beaten
½ cup boiled shrimp, finely chopped
½ cup mushrooms, finely chopped
2 truffles, minced
1 teaspoon Worcestershire sauce
2 teaspoons chopped parsley
1 dozen oysters

Fill two pie plates with rock salt and place in oven to preheat salt. While this is warming make sauce by melting butter in 9-inch saucepan over medium heat and sauteing onions until tender. Blend in the flour thoroughly. Cook slowly about 5 minutes, stirring constantly; do not brown. Remove from heat. Blend in fish stock, wine, salt and pepper until smooth. Blend in egg yolk thoroughly. Return pan to heat and gently cook while adding shrimp, mushrooms, truffles, Worcestershire sauce and parsley, about 15 minutes. Place a half dozen shells on each pie pan and fill each with an oyster. Put sauce in a pastry bag and cover each oyster with sauce. Top each with a sprinkling of paprika and bread crumbs. Dot with butter. Bake in a preheated oven 350° (moderate) 10 to 15 minutes, or until edges of oysters begin to curl. 2 servings.

OYSTERS CASINO

♉

1 cup chili sauce
1 cup catsup
⅓ cup horseradish
3 dozen oysters, parboiled in oyster water, reserving shells
9 strips bacon, cut in quarters

To make sauce, combine chili sauce, catsup and horseradish; heat through over slow fire. Place each warm parboiled oyster on half shell and cover each first with sauce, then with piece of bacon. Broil about 6 inches from flame until bacon is cooked. 6 servings.

CURRIED OYSTERS

❦

¼ *cup butter*
½ *cup minced onion*
¼ *cup finely chopped mushrooms*
½ *cup finely chopped boiled shrimp*
¼ *teaspoon powdered thyme*
¼ *cup flour*
1 *tablespoon curry powder*
1 *cup fish stock*
2 *cups milk*
3 *dozen oysters*

Fill 6 pie pans with rock salt and preheat in hot oven. While this is warming, make sauce by melting butter in large fry pan. Saute onion. Add mushrooms, shrimp, and thyme. Blend in flour and reduce heat. Cook, stirring until flour starts to discolor. Quickly stir in curry, stock and milk to a smooth consistency. Cook slowly until thickened. Place 6 half shells on each pie plate and place an oyster on each shell. Cover each oyster with curry sauce and sprinkle over with bread crumbs. Bake in preheated oven at 475° (very hot) for 5 minutes, or until oysters curl on edges. 6 servings.

OYSTERS J'AIME

🎭

½ cup chopped shallots
½ cup butter
¼ cup flour
⅓ cup catsup
2 tablespoons Worcestershire sauce
⅓ cup chili sauce
1 cup oyster water
1 cup sherry
1 cup mushrooms, sliced
¼ teaspoon salt
Dash cayenne
¼ teaspoon black pepper
24 oysters

In a 9-inch skillet saute shallots in butter. Blend in flour and stir until very brown, about 8 to 10 minutes. Blend in catsup, Worcestershire, and chili sauce. Stir in oyster water, sherry, mushrooms and seasonings. Simmer about 30 minutes over medium heat, adding oysters in last 10 minutes of cooking. Remove from heat and place in 4 casseroles (8 ounce size). Garnish with chopped parsley and serve piping hot. 4 servings.

OYSTERS PAN ROAST

♥

⅓ *cup chopped shallots*
½ *cup butter*
¼ *cup flour*
1 *cup oyster water (if needed, add water*
   to complete volume)
Dash cayenne
1 *dozen oysters*
1 *tablespoon grated Parmesan cheese*

In a 9-inch skillet over medium heat, saute shallots in butter. Blend in flour and cook slowly 3 to 5 minutes more. Blend in oyster water and cayenne, continue cooking until sauce begins to thicken. Add oysters and heat through. Remove from heat, put mixture into 8-ounce casseroles and sprinkle with Parmesan cheese. Pass under broiler about 2 minutes or until browned on top. 2 servings.

OYSTERS ROCKEFELLER

♟

1 cup chopped shallots
½ cup chopped parsley
1½ cups chopped young spinach
½ cup flour
1 cup melted butter
1 cup oyster water
2 cloves garlic, minced
½ teaspoon salt
¼ teaspoon cayenne
¼ cup minced anchovies
4 ounces absinthe
8 or 4 dozen oysters

Fill a pie pan with rock salt for each serving. Place in oven to pre-heat salt. While salt is heating, make sauce by putting shallots, parsley and spinach through food chopper. Stir flour into melted butter and cook 5 minutes: do not brown. Blend in oyster water, garlic, salt and cayenne. Stir in chopped greens and anchovies. Simmer, covered, 20 minutes. Remove cover, stir in absinthe and cook until thickened.

Place half shells (6 per serving) on hot rock salt. Fill each shell with an oyster. Put sauce in a pastry bag and cover each oyster. Bake in preheated 400° (moderately hot) oven for about 5 minutes or until edges of oysters begin to curl. 6 to 8 servings.

OYSTERS ROFFIGNAC

❦

¾ cup butter
⅓ cup finely chopped cooked mushrooms
⅓ cup finely chopped shallots
½ cup finely chopped onion
½ cup finely chopped boiled shrimp
2 tablespoons garlic, minced
2 tablespoons flour
½ teaspoon salt
⅛ teaspoon pepper
Dash cayenne
1 cup oyster water
½ cup red wine
2 dozen oysters

Fill four pie pans with rock salt and place in hot oven to preheat salt. While salt is warming make sauce. In a 9-inch skillet melt butter and lightly saute mushrooms, shallots, onion, shrimp and garlic. When onion is golden brown, add flour, salt, pepper and cayenne. Brown well, about 7 to 10 minutes. Blend in the oyster water and wine and simmer over low heat for 15 to 20 minutes. Place 6 half shells on each pie pan and place an oyster in each. Put stuffing in pastry bag and cover each oyster. Bake in preheated oven (moderately hot) 400° for 10 to 12 minutes or until edges of oysters begin to curl. 4 servings.

SHRIMP MARINIERE

½ cup butter
1 cup finely chopped shallots
3 tablespoons flour
2 cups milk
½ teaspoon salt
¼ teaspoon cayenne
⅓ cup white wine
1 pound boiled shrimp, peeled and veined
1 egg yolk, beaten

In a 9-inch skillet melt butter and saute shallots until tender. Blend in flour and cook slowly 3 to 5 minutes more, stirring constantly. Stir in milk until smooth. Add salt, pepper and wine. Cook about 10 minutes more. Remove from heat, add shrimp, and quickly stir in egg yolk. Return to heat and slowly cook until heated through. Place in ramekins and sprinkle tops with paprika and heat under broiler until piping hot. 3 to 4 servings.

SHRIMP REMOULADE

¾ cup minced parsley
¾ cup minced shallots
¾ cup minced celery
¾ cup minced dill pickle
1 tablespoon minced garlic
1¾ cup creole hot mustard
3 tablespoons horseradish
¼ cup vinegar
¼ cup salad oil

Mix all ingredients together and chill. This sauce will keep, if refrigerated, for many weeks. The more it stands the better the taste. For shrimp remoulade, marinate 6 large cooked shrimp in ½ cup sauce for each serving. Serve on bed of shredded greens.

STUFFED FAN-TAILED SHRIMPS

♎

3 lbs. large shrimp
½ cup butter
½ cup finely chopped green onions
3 cloves garlic, chopped
1 cup flour
1 pt. fish stock
3 egg yolks
Salt, pepper and bread crumbs

Saute onions and garlic in butter. Blend in flour. Add fish stock, and slowly stir in egg yolks, one at a time. Season and cook slowly 5–10 minutes.

Peel shrimp, leaving tail on. Partially split each shrimp from top to tail, and open, or spread out. Arrange shrimp in buttered baking pan, with one teaspoon of stuffing mixture on each shrimp. Sprinkle with bread crumbs, dot liberally with butter and bake in 350° oven for 25 minutes, or until shrimp are cooked. Serve with tartar sauce.

ESCARGOTS BORDELAISE

♥

8 canned snails in shell
¼ cup minced garlic
1 cup melted butter
½ cup sauterne
1 tablespoon parsley
Salt and pepper

First fill bottom of each shell with melted garlic butter. Put snails in shells and add more garlic butter.

In a 9-inch skillet over medium heat, saute snails in shells in butter and garlic about 5 minutes. Then add wine, salt and pepper. Serve in small dishes garnished with freshly chopped parsley. 2 servings.

SNAILS BOURGUIGNONNE

🐌

2 tablespoons butter
⅛ cup finely chopped onion
⅓ cup finely chopped shallots
2 tablespoons minced garlic
¼ cup flour
1 cup whole canned tomatoes
¼ cup liquid from snails
1 can (4½ oz. size) snails
¼ cup diced, cooked carrots
Salt and pepper to taste

In a 9-inch skillet over medium heat, melt butter and saute onion, shallots and garlic. Stir in flour and brown thoroughly over low heat. Blend in tomatoes and liquid from snails. Add snails, carrots, salt and pepper, cook slowly 10 to 15 minutes, stirring constantly. 2 servings.

SNAILS POULETTE

♉

⅓ *cup chopped shallots*
½ *cup butter*
¼ *cup flour*
½ *cup sliced boiled mushrooms*
1 cup fish stock
12 snails

Saute shallots in butter. Blend in flour and cook slowly 3 to 5 minutes more. Blend in fish stock and cook until sauce begins to thicken. Add snails and mushrooms and heat through. Serve on toast, garnished with paprika or parsley. 2 servings.

Soups

CONSOMME SHAW

❧

1 large onion, shredded
1 cup finely chopped celery
1 carrot, finely chopped
1 cup whole tomatoes
Whites of 6 eggs and the shells
2 teaspoons white pepper
Pinch cayenne
8 cups beef stock
3 bottles (8 oz. size) clam juice

Combine all ingredients, except clam juice, and simmer for 1½ hours. Remove from heat and strain. Heat clam juice and serve ½ clam juice to ½ hot consomme in soup cups. Garnish with parsley sprig.

JELLIED CONSOMME WITH SOUR CREAM

Follow recipe for Consomme Shaw omitting clam juice. While simmering add 2 tablespoons of dissolved gelatin. Chill thoroughly. To serve, break up consomme slightly with fork and pile into soup cups. Garnish generously with sour cream and serve.

CRAYFISH BISQUE

STUFFING

½ cup butter
1 cup chopped shallots
1 tablespoon flour
1 can tomatoes
1 cup bread crumbs
½ teaspoon salt
½ teaspoon pepper

SOUP

10 lbs. crayfish
1 cup butter
1 cup coarsely chopped onion
½ teaspoon minced garlic
1 cup chopped celery
1 cup chopped green onion
2 carrots sliced coarse
½ cup flour
5 cups fish stock
1 cup whole tomatoes
1 tablespoon paprika
4 bay leaves
1 teaspoon salt
½ teaspoon cayenne

Soak the 10 lbs. of crayfish ½ hour in cold water with 6 tablespoons of salt.

Saute onions, celery, carrots, and garlic in a cup of butter. Add flour, then tomatoes and a tablespoon paprika. Add bay leaves and fish stock.

Put all but 20 of the crayfish in a baking pan and crush as much as possible with a wooden mallet. Bake in 350° oven 15–20 minutes. Add to soup. Boil slowly for 25 minutes. Remove from heat and strain through coarse sieve and return to heat. Boil again 5 minutes. Strain again through fine sieve. If necessary add more water. Simmer while stuffing heads.

STUFFING

Take remaining 20 large crayfish and boil 5 minutes. Remove shells of heads and save. Take out all of the meat. Melt butter. Saute shallots; add flour, tomatoes and bread crumbs, and finely chopped crayfish tails. Salt and pepper to taste. Stuff into shells of heads.

Add to soup and simmer 5 minutes.

OYSTER STEW

❦

1 quart half milk, half cream
2 dozen oysters
½ teaspoon salt
⅛ teaspoon cayenne
1 pat butter

Combine all ingredients in saucepan and heat just to boiling. Reduce heat and simmer 5 minutes. 4 servings.

CREOLE GUMBO

♒

1 cup butter
1 cup finely chopped white onion
1 cup finely chopped celery
½ cup flour
4 cups liquid (add water to oyster water to make 1 quart)
2 cups whole canned tomatoes
3–4 bay leaves
3 dozen oysters
1 dozen crabs ⃰
2 cups raw shrimp, peeled and veined
3 cups okra, sliced thin
4 teaspoons salt
¾ teaspoon white pepper
Dash cayenne

Melt butter in a 4-quart saucepan over medium heat. Add celery and onion and saute until lightly browned. Stir in flour and cook to golden brown. Blend in liquid and tomatoes and simmer about 5 minutes. Add bay leaves, crabs, oysters, shrimp, okra, salt and pepper and continue cooking on low heat for 20 minutes. Serve with hot fluffy rice. Yield: about 2 quarts.

⃰ Scald live crabs. Clean, remove hard shell and legs, split crabs in half and crack claws.

ONION SOUP

1½ cups butter
4 cups sliced white onions
1¾ cups flour
12 cups beef stock
½ teaspoon cayenne
1½ tablespoons salt
1 egg yolk
2 tablespoons cream

In a six-quart soup kettle melt butter, add onions and reduce heat to very low, cooking until onions are melted down. Be careful not to brown onions in the first stages of cooking. Add flour and cook 5 to 10 minutes more, stirring occasionally. Blend in stock, salt and pepper and bring to boil. Reduce heat and simmer about 15 minutes. Remove kettle from heat. Beat together egg yolk and cream, add a little of the soup and mix quickly, then add to soup kettle. Serve in soup cups with toasted rounds of bread or croutons and sprinkle with grated Parmesan cheese, buttered bread crumbs. Brown under broiler flame and serve. Yield: 3 quarts soup.

OYSTER SOUP

¥

½ *cup butter*
1 cup finely chopped celery
1 cup finely chopped shallots
1 tablespoon flour
1 teaspoon chopped garlic
Oyster water plus water to make 6 cups
2 dozen large oysters
2 bay leaves
Salt and pepper to taste

Melt butter in saucepan; saute celery and shallots until tender. Blend in flour and cook 5 minutes more, stirring over low heat. Add remaining ingredients and simmer 20 minutes. Remove bay leaves and serve. Yield: 1½ quarts.

RED BEAN SOUP

✢

1 cup red kidney beans
1 cup butter
1 cup chopped white onion
1 cup chopped celery
1 cup flour
6 cups beef stock
½ teaspoon pepper

Cover washed kidney beans with water and soak overnight. In a 4-quart saucepan melt butter and saute onion and celery for 10 minutes. Blend in flour, add stock and beans. Boil slowly 1½–2 hours until beans are very tender. Strain, mashing beans through strainer. Reheat and season. Yield: 1½ quarts.

C R E M E   D E   S E N E G A L E S E

❧

½ *cup butter*
½ *cup flour*
2 *teaspoons curry powder*
8 *cups hot milk*
2 *tablespoons Lea & Perrins sauce*
1 *teaspoon salt*
½ *teaspoon cayenne*
Chopped parsley

In a 4-quart saucepan melt butter and stir in flour, cooking over low heat for 10 to 12 minutes, but do not brown. Blend in curry powder and cook 1 to 2 minutes more, stirring constantly. Slowly add milk, stirring to keep smooth. Add Lea & Perrins, salt and pepper, simmer 10 minutes. Remove from heat; strain. Serve hot or cold garnished with chopped parsley. Yield: 2 quarts.

TURTLE SOUP AU SHERRY

4 pounds turtle meat, boiled and cut into small cubes *
1 cup butter
3 cups chopped white onion
1 cup flour
½ cup tomato puree
10 cups turtle stock *
1 cup sherry
½ cup Lea & Perrins sauce
3 hard cooked eggs, finely chopped
1 cup finely chopped parsley
1 lemon, thinly sliced

In a soup kettle, over medium heat, melt butter, add onions and saute until transparent. Stir in flour and cook until browned. Add tomato puree and cook 5 minutes more. Add stock, sherry and Lea & Perrins, continue cooking slowly 15 minutes. Add turtle meat and egg, simmer 10 to 15 minutes more. Remove from heat, stir in parsley and lemon slices. Serve at once. Yield: About 3 quarts.

* In a large kettle cover turtle meat with 4 quarts water, 2 bay leaves, 2 teaspoons cayenne, 2 tablespoons salt, bring to boil and cook until turtle meat is very tender. Add more water if needed to keep liquid to about 3 quarts. Strain and reserve stock. Cut meat into small cubes.

V I C H Y S S O I S E

❦

6 *large potatoes*
1 *sliced onion*
½ *stalk celery coarsely chopped*
1 *cup diced ham, or small ham bone*
½ *cup shallots*
4 *cups milk*
1 *cup cream*
1 *tablespoon Worcestershire sauce*
Dash of cayenne
Salt to taste

Peel potatoes and cut in quarters. Put in pot and cover with a liberal amount of water. Add ham, onions and celery. Boil until potatoes fall to pieces. Add water if necessary. Remove from heat and add milk and cream gradually, while stirring. Strain. Add ½ cup finely chopped shallots. Season and chill. Serve cold.

WATER CRESS SOUP

🦞

1 cup butter
1 large white onion, chopped
1 cup chopped celery with a few leaves
1 cup flour
9 cups beef stock
1 teaspoon salt
½ teaspoon pepper
1½ cups chopped water cress

Melt butter in a large saucepan; saute onion and celery until very tender. Stir in flour and continue cooking over low heat 8 to 10 minutes, stirring constantly. Blend in beef stock, salt and pepper. Simmer 30 minutes. Strain. Stir in water cress. Yield: 2 quarts.

Seafood

B O U I L L A B A I S E   M A R S E I L L A I S E

½ *cup butter*
1 *cup minced white onion*
½ *cup shallots*
1 *teaspoon minced garlic*
1 *cup whole raw shrimp, peeled*
2 *dozen raw oysters*
½ *cup cooked chopped lobster meat*
½ *cup whole raw crayfish tails, peeled*
1 *tablespoon flour*
1 *cup whole tomatoes*
1 *teaspoon salt*
½ *teaspoon cayenne*
2 *cups fish stock (from Redfish head and bones)*
4–5 *lb. Redfish*
1 *lemon, sliced*
Pinch saffron

In a large pan melt butter and saute onion, shallots and garlic until tender. Add shrimp, oysters, lobster and crayfish * and continue cooking a few minutes more. Stir in flour and cook 3–5 minutes longer. Add tomatoes, salt, pepper and fish stock and cook slowly 20 minutes. Add saffron and simmer 5 minutes more. Remove from heat. While above sauce is cooking, tenderloin Redfish (taking out bones and removing skin and head). Cut in 4 pieces and place in baking pan. Bake in preheated oven 350° 15 minutes, or until fish is done. Put Redfish in soup bowl, pour sauce over it, and garnish with sliced lemon. 4 servings.

* Other seafoods may be substituted, i.e. soft shell crab, legs and claws removed, and grilled on both sides 1 minute.

BUSTERS BERNAISE*

9 busters, cleaned and dried
1 egg, beaten
1 cup milk
½ cup butter
6 buttered toast triangles
1½ cups Bearnaise Sauce (page 185)
1 tablespoon chopped parsley

Dip busters in batter of 1 beaten egg and 1 cup milk. Drain. Dredge in flour and fry in butter until golden brown. Mount on toast triangles and cover with Bearnaise Sauce. Sprinkle with parsley. 3 servings.

* "Buster" is the name given to the crab when it is in the stage between hard and soft shell.

CRAB MEAT MARINIERE

❦

½ cup butter
1 cup finely chopped shallots
3 tablespoons flour
2 cups milk
½ teaspoon salt
¼ teaspoon cayenne
⅓ cup white wine
1½ cups crab meat
1 egg yolk, beaten

In a 9-inch skillet melt butter. Saute shallots until tender. Blend in flour and cook slowly 3 to 5 minutes, stirring constantly. Stir in milk until smooth. Add salt, pepper, and wine. Cook about 10 minutes more. Add crab meat and heat through. Remove from heat and quickly beat in egg yolk. Spoon into 8-ounce casseroles, sprinkle with paprika. Heat under broiler flame and serve piping hot. 3 to 4 servings.

CRAB MEAT RAVIGOTTE

♋

2 tablespoons butter
2 tablespoons flour
½ teaspoon salt
Dash cayenne
1 cup milk
⅓ cup chopped boiled green pepper
⅓ cup coarsely chopped pimiento
1 tablespoon capers
1 teaspoon tarragon vinegar
1 cup lump crab meat
⅓ cup Hollandaise Sauce (page 190)

In a saucepan melt butter and stir in flour, salt and cayenne. Blend in milk and cook, stirring constantly, over low heat until sauce begins to thicken. Add green pepper, pimiento, capers, tarragon vinegar, and crab meat. Heat through on low heat. Remove from heat and fold in Hollandaise Sauce. Serve in 8-ounce casseroles or on Holland rusks. Garnish with paprika and chopped parsley. 2 servings.

STUFFED CRAB

♉

½ cup butter
1 medium onion, finely chopped
½ cup finely chopped shallots
2 cups coarse bread crumbs dampened
     with oyster water or fish stock
2 bay leaves
½ teaspoon salt
½ teaspoon black pepper
Dash cayenne
½ pound crab meat
1 tablespoon chopped parsley
½ cup buttered bread crumbs

In a 9-inch skillet over medium heat, melt butter, saute onion and shallots until tender. Add dampened bread crumbs and continue cooking 3 to 5 minutes. Add bay leaves, salt, pepper, cayenne, crab meat and parsley, mix thoroughly and heat through. Remove skillet from heat. Remove bay leaves. Pack stuffing into 4 crab shells and cover with buttered bread crumbs. Arrange shells on shallow baking dish and bake at 350° (moderate oven) for 15 to 20 minutes. 4 servings.

CRAYFISH ÉTOUFÉE

1 cup butter
1 cup finely chopped white onion
½ cup finely chopped celery
1 cup finely chopped shallots
1 teaspoon minced garlic
2 tablespoons flour
1 cup whole tomatoes
2 cups fish stock
2 teaspoons salt
1 teaspoon black pepper
Dash cayenne
1 tablespoon Worcestershire sauce
1½ cups crayfish meats

In a large saucepan melt butter and saute onion, celery and shallots until tender. Add garlic and cook 1 minute more. Stir in flour and stir constantly until golden brown. Add tomatoes and brown. Blend in stock and simmer 10 minutes. Add salt, pepper, cayenne, Worcestershire sauce and crayfish, cook slowly 15 to 20 minutes, stirring occasionally. Serve with hot fluffy rice. 3 to 4 servings.

FLOUNDER COLBERT

6 flounder filets
½ cup butter
1 chopped onion
½ cup flour
½ cup tomato puree
1 pt. fish stock
1 cup Burgundy wine
1 tablespoon lemon juice
1 teaspoon Worcestershire sauce
2 eggs
½ pt. milk
1 cup vegetable oil
Salt, pepper and bread crumbs

Saute onions in butter. Blend in flour, add tomato puree, and then fish stock, wine, lemon juice, Worchestershire sauce, and simmer 5–10 minutes. Season flounder filets with salt and pepper, roll in flour, and dip in preparation of beaten eggs and milk. Roll in bread crumbs and fry in oil until golden brown. Serve flounder on top of sauce, garnished with lemon slices. Serves 6.

FLOUNDER GRENOBLAISE

2 pounds filet of flounder
½ cup butter
Juice of 2 lemons
1 tablespoon Worcestershire sauce
1 tablespoon chopped parsley
¼ cup capers

Salt and pepper flounder to taste and dip into batter of 1 beaten egg and 1 cup of milk. Drain. Dredge fish in flour. Melt butter in 9-inch skillet and saute flounder until golden brown. Add lemon juice, Worcestershire sauce, parsley and capers, heat through. 2 servings.

STUFFED FLOUNDER

♋

STUFFING

3 tablespoons butter
¼ cup finely chopped green onions
¼ cup flour
¾ cup fish stock
3 tablespoons white wine
¼ teaspoon salt
Dash cayenne
1 egg yolk, beaten
⅓ cup crab meat
½ cup boiled shrimp, peeled and veined
½ dozen oysters, lightly blanched
2 teaspoons finely chopped parsley
6 tablespoons paprika
5 tablespoons parmesan cheese
3 tablespoons bread crumbs
¼ cup vegetable oil

2 flounders (1½ pounds each)

Over medium heat in 9-inch skillet, melt butter and saute onions until tender. Blend in the flour thoroughly. Cook slowly about 5 minutes stirring constantly: do not brown. Remove skillet from heat. Blend in fish stock, wine, salt and pepper, until smooth. Blend in egg yolk thoroughly. Return pan to heat and gently cook over low heat, stirring constantly, about 15 minutes. Add crab meat, shrimp, oysters and parsley and mix thoroughly, heat through and remove from heat.

How to prepare flounders: Cut head from fish, with fish lying flat, dark side up, make a slit from head to tail with boning knife, going through flesh to bone. Now with tail section of fish toward you, take a boning knife and work from center slit to fins loosening the flesh from the bone. Turn fish so that tail is now away from you and insert blade of knife under backbone. Work from center to side in a slicing motion to loosen back of fish from bone. With a scissors, cut bone loose from fins. Now lift backbone and break away from fish near tail. Your flounder is ready for the stuffing prepared above. Fill with stuffing and sprinkle with a mixture of 6 tablespoons paprika, 5 tablespoons parmesan cheese and 3 tablespoons bread crumbs. Close fish. In large (12-in.) cast-iron skillet sear flounders in ¼ cup vegetable oil. Place skillet with flounders into 400° (mod. hot oven) about 20 min. or until done. Serve with lemon slices and parsley. 2 servings.

FROG LEGS PROVENÇALE

½ cup butter
¼ cup green pepper, chopped
½ cup chopped onions
2 teaspoons minced garlic
½ cup sliced mushrooms
1 tablespoon chopped parsley
2 tablespoons chopped shallots
2 cups whole tomatoes
½ teaspoon salt
Dash cayenne
1 egg, slightly beaten
1 cup milk
8 frog legs

Melt butter in a 10-inch skillet. Saute green pepper, garlic, mushrooms, parsley, onions and shallots. Add tomatoes, salt and pepper and simmer over very low heat 10 minutes. While sauce is cooking, make a batter of the egg and milk. Dip frog legs in this batter and drain. Dredge in flour and fry in butter until golden brown. Add to sauce and simmer five minutes more. Arrange legs on serving platter and cover with sauce. 2 servings.

L O B S T E R   D U M A S

❦

¼ cup butter
⅓ cup sliced mushrooms
1 cup finely chopped shallots
2 tablespoons minced garlic
2 cups chopped lobster meat
2 tablespoons flour
1½ cups fish stock
1 tablespoon Worcestershire sauce
¾ teaspoon salt
⅛ teaspoon cayenne
⅓ cup Burgundy
1 bay leaf

Melt butter in 9-inch skillet over medium heat and saute mushrooms, shallots, garlic and lobster until tender. Stir in flour thoroughly and continue cooking, stirring constantly until golden brown. Blend in fish stock, Worcestershire sauce, salt, cayenne and wine until smooth. Add bay leaf, continue cooking over low heat, stirring until heated through. 2 servings.

LOBSTER NEWBURG

2 cups diced lobster
1½ cups cream
½ teaspoon salt
¼ teaspoon cayenne
½ cup sherry
2 egg yolks, beaten

In a saucepan combine lobster, cream, salt and pepper. Slowly heat to boiling point. Mix sherry and egg yolk. Blend into hot mixture, stirring constantly over low heat until thickened. Spoon into 8-ounce casseroles and sprinkle with paprika. 4 servings.

L O B S T E R   T H E R M I D O R

❦

1 lobster about 3 pounds
⅓ cup butter
1 cup finely chopped shallots
2 tablespoons flour
1½ cups cream
½ cup sliced boiled mushrooms
½ teaspoon salt
¼ teaspoon cayenne
½ cup sherry
2 egg yolks, beaten

Boil lobster in salted water. Drain; split in half lengthwise, remove lobster meat, coarsely chop. Wash and retain shell.

In a 9-inch skillet melt butter and saute shallots. Stir in flour and cook 3 to 5 minutes over low heat. Blend in cream, stirring until smooth, salt and cayenne. Beat sherry and egg yolks together and stir quickly into hot mixture. Add lobster meat and mushrooms and heat through. Fill lobster shell generously with this mixture and cover with buttered bread crumbs. Sprinkle with paprika. Broil until browned, about 5 minutes. 2 servings.

POMPANO GRAND DUC

♥

3 tablespoons butter
¼ cup finely chopped green onions
¼ cup flour
¾ cup fish stock
3 tablespoons white wine
¼ teaspoon salt
Dash cayenne
1 egg yolk, beaten
2 cups seasoned mashed potatoes
6 warm green asparagus spears
1½ pounds poached filet of pompano
      (save head, skin and bones for stock)
6 each boiled shrimp and scalded oysters
½ cup Hollandaise Sauce (page 190)
½ cup unsweetened whipped cream

Over medium heat in 7-inch skillet, melt butter and saute onions until tender. Blend in flour thoroughly. Cook slowly about 5 minutes stirring constantly, do not brown. Remove from heat. Blend in fish stock, wine, salt and pepper until smooth. Blend in egg yolk thoroughly. Return pan to heat and gently cook over low heat, stirring constantly, about 15 minutes. Remove from heat and keep warm.

With mashed potatoes in pastry bag, flute a wall around extreme edge of large, warm platter. In center of platter place bundle of asparagus. Cover with fish sauce, made above, and arrange pompano on this bed of fish sauce. Garnish pompano with shrimp and oysters. Combine Hollandaise Sauce and whipped cream and pour over fish. Bake at 375° (quick moderate oven) until potatoes brown lightly on edges. 3 to 4 servings.

P O M P A N O   E N   P A P I L L O T E

♃

Parchment paper
3 tablespoons butter
¼ cup finely chopped green onion
¼ cup flour
¾ cup fish stock
3 tablespoons white wine
¼ teaspoon salt
Dash cayenne
1 egg yolk, beaten
½ cup boiled shrimp, peeled
½ dozen oysters, blanched
1 teaspoon chopped parsley
1 rolled filet of pompano or trout poached in
     salted water * (about ¾ pound)*

Fold a 20″ square of parchment paper in half and cut a large heart. This will be your papillote.

In a 9-inch skillet over medium heat, melt butter and saute onion until tender. Blend in the flour thoroughly. Cook slowly about 5 minutes, stirring constantly: do not brown. Remove skillet from heat. Blend in fish stock, wine, salt and pepper until smooth. Blend in egg yolk thoroughly. Return pan to heat and gently cook over low heat, stirring constantly about 15 minutes. Add shrimp, oysters and parsley and heat through.

On center of one inside half of parchment "heart" place half of above mixture, and place rolled pompano or trout on the sauce mixture. Top this with the other half of the sauce mixture. Fold the top half of the paper over and starting at the arc (opposite

---

* One 2-pound pompano or trout will render two ¾-pound filets after cleaning and boning. Save head and bones to make fish stock.

point) fold the two ends of the paper together like sealing pie dough. Continue this folding seam around to the tip. Pinch the last fold tightly. Place papillote on shallow baking dish. Bake in a pre-heated oven 350° (moderate) 10 to 15 minutes or until paper is golden brown. 1 serving.

POMPANO PONTCHARTRAIN AMANDINE

1½ pounds pompano with head
1 buster *
1 egg
1 cup milk
½ cup butter
⅓ cup slivered almonds
Juice of 2 lemons
2 tablespoons Worcestershire sauce
1 tablespoon chopped parsley

Thoroughly wash and dry the fish and the buster. Make a batter of the egg and milk. Dip both the fish and the buster into this batter and drain. Dredge in seasoned flour. In a large skillet, melt butter and saute the fish and the buster until tender and golden brown. Remove first the fish to a warm serving platter and then the buster which must be placed across the head of the fish on a diagonal. Add almonds to skillet and brown. Add lemon juice, Worcestershire sauce and parsley, heat through and pour over fish. 1 serving.

* Or substitute 3 boiled shrimp and 3 scalded oysters, if busters are not available.

REDFISH COURTBOUILLON

❧

½ cup vegetable oil
1 cup chopped celery
2 cups chopped green pepper
1¾ cups chopped white onion
1 cup finely chopped shallots
2 tablespoons minced garlic
4 bay leaves
¾ teaspoon powdered thyme
3 cups whole canned tomatoes
¼ teaspoon black pepper
2 teaspoons salt
½ teaspoon cayenne
2 tablespoons paprika
4 cups fish stock
3 tablespoons lemon juice
¾ cup Burgundy
4 pound Redfish (clean and filet fish,
    using bones, skin and head for making stock)
1 lemon, sliced

In a large pot or large deep skillet heat oil and saute next five ingredients. Stir in bay leaves, thyme, tomatoes, pepper, salt, cayenne and paprika, simmer 5 minutes more. Stir in stock and cook slowly 25 to 30 minutes. While this is cooking, lightly coat Redfish with seasoned flour and sear on both sides on hot grill, lower heat and continue cooking fish until almost done. Remove from heat and keep fish warm. When first mixture has cooked for approximately 30 minutes, stir in lemon juice and Burgundy. Add fish and cook slowly 10 to 12 minutes more. Add lemon slices and serve. Good with hot fluffy rice. 4 to 5 servings.

REDFISH GELPI

½ cup butter
¾ cup finely chopped shallots
¼ cup chopped parboiled green pepper
1 teaspoon minced garlic
¼ cup chopped pimiento
1 tablespoon capers
1 teaspoon tarragon vinegar
1 teaspoon Worcestershire sauce
1 teaspoon salt
¼ teaspoon cayenne
½ cup fish stock
1 tablespoon parsley, chopped
4 pounds Redfish, tenderloined

In a 9-inch skillet melt butter and saute shallots, green pepper, garlic until tender. Add pimiento, capers, vinegar, Worcestershire sauce, salt, pepper, and fish stock. Simmer 10 minutes. Add parsley, stir. Remove from heat. Broil Redfish until done and place on platter. Cover with sauce. 2 servings.

RED SNAPPER HOLLANDAISE

❦

4 teaspoons salt
2 bay leaves
1 lemon, sliced
1 onion, sliced
Dash cayenne
2 quarts water
4 pounds Red Snapper, cleaned and tenderloined
2 cups Hollandaise Sauce (page 190)
2 tablespoons chopped parsley

Combine first six ingredients and poach Red Snapper, about 15 minutes. Remove from water, drain well, place on serving platter. Cover with Hollandaise Sauce and chopped parsley. Garnish with lemon slices. 2 to 3 servings.

SHRIMP CLEMENCEAU

¼ cup butter
½ cup sliced mushrooms
1 teaspoon minced garlic
1 cup potatoes, cubed, deep fried light brown, and drained on absorbent paper
2 lbs. seasoned boiled shrimp, peeled and veined
1 cup small green peas
1 teaspoon minced parsley

In a 9-inch skillet melt butter and saute mushrooms, garlic, and potatoes 8 to 10 minutes. Add shrimp and saute 5 to 10 minutes more. Add peas and parsley, heat through and serve. 2 servings.

SHRIMP CREOLE

❧

½ *cup vegetable oil*
1 cup coarsely chopped green pepper
2 cups coarsely chopped onion
1 cup chopped celery
2 teaspoons minced garlic
2 cups whole tomatoes
1 tablespoon paprika
¼ *teaspoon cayenne*
1 teaspoon salt
3 cups water
1 bay leaf
3 pounds raw shrimp, peeled and veined
2 tablespoons cornstarch

Heat vegetable oil and saute next 4 ingredients until tender. Add tomatoes and brown. Stir in paprika, cayenne, salt and water. Add bay leaf and simmer 15 minutes. Add shrimp and continue simmering 10 to 12 minutes more. If desired, thicken sauce with cornstarch mixed in a little cold water. Serve with hot fluffy rice. 4 to 6 servings.

SHRIMP CURRY

♥

⅓ cup butter
½ cup minced white onion
¼ teaspoon salt
Dash each white pepper and cayenne
1 crumbled bay leaf
Pinch of powdered thyme
1½ tablespoons curry powder
1½ tablespoons flour
1¾ cups fish stock
2 allspice
2 cups boiled shrimp, peeled and veined

In a saucepan melt butter and saute onion until golden. Add salt, pepper, cayenne, bay leaf, thyme, curry and flour, blend well and stir while cooking 10 minutes more. Blend in fish stock. Remove from heat. Put mixture through blender to puree. Return to heat and add allspice, and shrimp. Continue cooking 5 minutes more. Remove allspice and serve curry on mounds of hot fluffy rice. Add chutney at side of serving dish if desired. 4 to 5 servings.

TROUT AMANDINE I

♧

2 pounds filet of trout
1 egg
1 cup milk
Flour
½ cup butter
⅓ cup slivered almonds
Juice of 2 lemons
2 tablespoons Worcestershire sauce
1 tablespoon chopped parsley

Salt and pepper trout. Dip in batter of 1 beaten egg and 1 cup milk. Drain. Dredge in flour. In 9-inch skillet melt butter and saute trout about 5 to 8 minutes, or until golden brown. Remove trout to warm platter. Add almonds to skillet and brown lightly. Add lemon juice, Worcestershire sauce and parsley, heat through and pour over fish. 3 to 4 servings.

TROUT AMANDINE II

🌱

6 filets of trout (½ lb. each)
2 eggs
½ pt. milk
Flour
2 cups vegetable oil
1 lb. almonds
1 cup butter
1 lemon
1 tablespoon chopped parsley
1 teaspoon Worcestershire sauce

Season trout filets with salt and pepper and roll in flour. Dip in milk, into which eggs are beaten. Fry slowly in deep fat until golden brown. Remove fish from fat and cover with crushed almonds.

Brown butter until golden brown and remove from heat. Squeeze lemon into butter, add Worcestershire sauce and parsley, pour over fish and serve. Serves 6.

TROUT BLANGÉ

❧

½ cup butter
1 tablespoon minced garlic
¾ cup raw shrimp, peeled
¾ cup raw oysters
½ cup sliced cooked mushrooms
½ teaspoon Spanish saffron
2 cups whole canned tomatoes
1 cup fish stock
¼ teaspoon cayenne
1 teaspoon salt
2 tablespoons cornstarch
¼ cup water
2 trout (2 lbs. each) cleaned, boned
*   (Save heads, skin and bones for making stock)*
2 cups seasoned mashed potatoes

In a 10-inch skillet melt butter and saute garlic, shrimp, oysters, mushrooms and saffron. Add tomatoes, fish stock, cayenne and salt. Simmer 15 to 20 minutes. Combine cornstarch and water, add to sauce to thicken. When desired consistency is obtained, remove pan from heat and add parsley. Keep warm. Grill or broil trout to a golden brown and remove to warm serving platter. Place mashed potatoes in a pastry bag and flute a wall around extreme edge of platter. Cover fish with warm sauce. Garnish with whole mushrooms and shrimp. Sprinkle potatoes with paprika. Place under flame until potatoes are lightly browned. 4 servings.

TROUT MARGUERY

🦃

2 half-pound filets of trout
½ cup warm boiled shrimp, peeled
½ cup boiled fresh mushroom caps
1 tablespoon chopped truffle
1 cup Hollandaise Sauce (page 190)

Roll up filet and poach in salted water. Remove from water and drain. Place fish in center of serving plate. Fold shrimp, mushrooms and truffles into Hollandaise Sauce and pour over trout. Garnish with parsley. 2 servings.

POACHED TROUT MARINIERE

❧

½ *cup butter*
1 *cup finely chopped shallots*
3 *tablespoons flour*
2 *cups milk*
½ *teaspoon salt*
¼ *teaspoon cayenne*
⅓ *cup white wine*
4 *half-pound filets of trout, poached* * *in salted water*
2 *egg yolks, beaten*

In a 9-inch skillet melt butter. Saute shallots until tender. Blend in flour and cook slowly 3 to 4 minutes, stirring constantly. Stir in milk until smooth. Add salt, pepper and wine. Cook about 10 minutes more. Add poached trout and heat through. Remove from heat and stir in egg yolks. Place pieces of warm poached trout in serving dish and spoon hot sauce over top. Sprinkle with paprika and heat under broiler flame until piping hot. 4 servings.

* Differs from boiling in that very little water is used, barely covering fish. Wine and vinegar, or lemon juice may be added.

T R O U T   N O R M A N D Y

❧

3 *two-pound filets of trout (½ lb. per serving)*
4 *oz. butter*
½ *cup chopped green onions*
½ *cup flour*
2½ *cups fish stock*
1 *cup white wine*
1 *lb. boiled shrimp*
3 *hard boiled eggs*
1 *tablespoon lemon juice*
1 *tablespoon capers*
1 *tablespoon Worcestershire sauce*
Salt, pinch of cayenne pepper, chopped parsley

Saute onions in butter. Blend in flour, gradually add fish stock, lemon juice, Worcestershire sauce, and wine. Boil 5 minutes. Add chopped shrimp, chopped hard boiled eggs and capers to sauce, and season with salt and cayenne.

Boil filets of trout 6–8 minutes. Arrange on platter and cover with sauce. Garnish with sliced lemons, sprinkle with parsley and serve. Serves 6.

T R O U T   V I N   B L A N C

2 half-pound filets of trout, poached (save head,
    skin and bones for making stock)
½ cup butter
1 cup finely chopped shallots
¼ cup flour
2 cups fish stock
½ teaspoon salt
Dash cayenne
1 egg yolk
½ cup sauterne
2 cups seasoned mashed potatoes

While trout is poaching in salted water, start sauce. Melt butter in a 9-inch skillet and saute shallots. Blend in flour and cook 5 minutes more. Blend in fish stock, salt and cayenne. Slowly heat to just below boiling point. Beat egg yolk and sauterne together and quickly stir into hot mixture. Heat through, remove from heat. With mashed potatoes in a pastry bag, make a wall at extreme edge of large platter. Drain fish and place on platter. Cover with sauce and garnish with oysters and shrimp, if desired. Sprinkle with paprika and broil until potatoes brown lightly on edges. 2 servings.

Fowl

CHICKEN CLEMENCEAU

❦

¼ *cup butter*
½ *cup boiled mushrooms*
1 *teaspoon minced garlic*
1 *cup potatoes, cubed small, deep fried light brown,*
     and drained on absorbent paper
1 *small chicken cut in pieces*
1 *cup small green peas*
1 *teaspoon minced parsley*

In a 9-inch skillet melt butter and saute chicken until done. Add mushrooms, garlic and potatoes and saute 5–10 minutes more. Add peas and parsley and heat through. Remove chicken to platter and cover with vegetable mixture. 2 servings.

CHICKEN FINANCIERE

♥

1 ready-to-cook chicken (2 pounds) disjointed
½ cup vegetable oil
½ cup coarsely chopped chicken livers
½ minced green onion
1 teaspoon minced garlic
1 tablespoon flour
1½ cups chicken stock
½ cup red wine
½ cup sliced mushrooms
¼ cup sliced olives
½ teaspoon salt
Dash cayenne
1 tablespoon Worcestershire

Dredge chicken pieces in seasoned flour. In a large skillet heat vegetable oil and fry chicken to golden brown and tender. Remove chicken to platter and keep warm. Saute chicken livers, green onion and garlic. Blend in flour and brown. Stir in chicken stock until smooth. Add remaining ingredients. Simmer 15 minutes. Return chicken to pan and continue to simmer 10 minutes more. 2 to 3 servings.

C H I C K E N F L O R E N T I N E

❦

2 cups seasoned mashed potatoes
1 cup warm creamed spinach
6 slices chicken breast
2 tablespoons butter
2 tablespoons flour
½ teaspoon salt
Dash cayenne
1 cup milk
2 tablespoons grated Parmesan cheese
1 teaspoon paprika
Butter

On two small platters, make a wall around extreme edge with potatoes in pastry bag. Make a bed in the center of each with creamed spinach. Cover spinach with sliced chicken. In a small heavy saucepan, melt the 2 tablespoons butter. Stir in flour, salt and pepper. Add milk gradually and stir constantly until thickened. Reduce heat and cook one or two minutes more. Pour this sauce over chicken. Sprinkle sauce with cheese. Sprinkle potatoes with paprika. Dot with butter and broil until sauce and potatoes brown lightly. 2 servings.

C H I C K E N   L I V E R S   S T .   P I E R R E

♉

½ *cup butter*
½ *cup chopped green pepper*
½ *cup chopped green onion*
½ *cup finely sliced white onion*
1½ *cups chicken livers*
2 *tablespoons chopped mushrooms*
½ *cup lima beans, cooked and drained*
¼ *cup sliced pimiento*
1 *teaspoon salt*
Dash cayenne

In a 9-inch skillet melt butter and saute green pepper, green onion, white onion. Add chicken livers and saute until browned, 8 to 10 minutes. Add mushrooms, lima beans, pimiento, salt and pepper. Heat through. 2 servings.

C H I C K E N   E N   P A P I L L O T E

3–4 lb. chicken
Parchment paper
½ cup butter
1 cup finely chopped green onion
1 cup flour
4 cups chicken stock
1 cup white wine
Salt to taste
Dash cayenne
3 beaten egg yolks
1 cup sliced boiled mushrooms
1 tablespoon chopped parsley

Fold a 20-inch square of parchment paper in half and cut a large heart. This will be your papillote. Make one for each serving.

Boil chicken, reserving stock. Melt butter in a skillet over medium heat and saute onion until tender. Blend in the flour thoroughly. Cook slowly about 5 minutes, stirring constantly. Do not brown. Removing skillet from heat, blend in chicken stock, wine, salt and pepper until smooth. Blend in egg yolk thoroughly. Return pan to heat and gently cook over low heat, stirring constantly about 15 minutes. Add diced leg meat from chicken, mushrooms and parsley and heat through.

On center of one inside half of parchment "heart" place 2 tablespoons of above mixture, then 2 slices breast of chicken, then 2 more tablespoons sauce mixture on top. Fold the top half of the paper over and starting at the arc (opposite point) fold the two ends of the paper together like sealing pie dough. Continue this folding seam around to the tip. Pinch the last fold tightly. Place papillote on shallow baking dish. Bake in a preheated oven 350° 10–15 minutes or until paper is golden brown. 4 servings.

CHICKEN PERIGORD

⚜

⅓ cup butter
½ cup minced shallots
1 cup chopped chicken livers
1 teaspoon minced truffle
1 egg
¼ cup red wine
½ teaspoon salt
Dash cayenne
¾ cup bread crumbs, dampened
1 ready-to-cook chicken (2½ pounds) or rock hens
1 tablespoon flour
1 cup chicken stock
1 teaspoon Worcestershire sauce
¼ cup red wine
1 tablespoon brandy
1 tablespoon minced truffle

Melt butter in skillet and saute shallots and chicken livers. Add truffle. Remove from heat. Beat egg and wine together and stir into hot mixture quickly. Add salt, pepper and bread crumbs. Mix thoroughly. Return to heat and stir while heating through. Stuff chicken and brush with melted butter. Bake in preheated oven 350° (moderate) 1½ to 2 hours. Remove chicken from pan. Add flour to drippings and brown. Blend in chicken stock until smooth. Add remaining ingredients and simmer 10 minutes. 2 servings.

CHICKEN POMPADOUR

♥

1 ready-to-cook chicken (2½ to 3 pounds), disjointed
½ cup butter or chicken fat
½ cup chopped green onion
⅓ cup flour
2 cups chicken stock
½ teaspoon salt
Dash cayenne
1 tablespoon Worcestershire sauce
⅓ cup sauterne

2 tomatoes
2 tablespoons vegetable oil
¼ cup minced shallots
¼ cup finely chopped onion
¼ cup finely chopped celery
¼ teaspoon powdered thyme
¼ pound ground beef
1 egg yolk
¼ teaspoon salt
Dash pepper
10 ounces broccoli, cooked
10 ounces asparagus spears, cooked
1½ cups small whole new potatoes, cooked
2 tablespoons chopped parsley
4 strips bacon grilled crisp

Dredge chicken pieces in seasoned flour. In large skillet melt butter or chicken fat and fry chicken until tender and brown. Place on large serving platter and keep warm.

Add butter to drippings to make ⅓ cup. Saute onion until tender. Blend in flour and brown. Stir in stock until smooth, add salt, pepper and Worcestershire sauce, simmer 10 minutes. Add sauterne and simmer 5 minutes more. While this is cooking make stuffing for tomatoes.

Scoop out centers of tomatoes, retaining quantity removed. In a small skillet heat vegetable oil and saute shallots, onion, celery and thyme. Add ground beef and stir to break up. Beef should be nice and brown. Add pieces of tomato scooped out earlier and saute a few minutes longer. Quickly stir in egg yolk, salt and pepper, heat through. Stuff tomatoes and broil 10 to 12 minutes.

Cook broccoli according to package directions (if frozen) and drain. Cook asparagus according to package directions (if frozen), drain. Roll new potatoes in melted butter and then in chopped parsley.

Now garnish platter of chicken in this manner. Cover chicken with warm sauce. Place broiled stuffed tomato at each end. Along one side of chicken make and arrange a bundle of half the broccoli, half the asparagus, and in between these, ¾ cup of the boiled potatoes. Duplicate the arrangement along the other side of the platter. Add bacon. 2 servings.

CHICKEN MARCHAND DE VIN

♟

1 ready-to-cook chicken (2½ to 3 pounds), disjointed
½ cup vegetable oil or chicken fat
2 cups Marchand de Vin Sauce (page 191)

Dredge chicken pieces in seasoned flour. Heat oil or chicken fat in large skillet and fry chicken until golden brown and tender. Place chicken pieces in a casserole and cover with hot Marchand de Vin Sauce. Bake in preheated oven 350° (moderate) 20 to 25 minutes. 2 to 3 servings.

CHICKEN PONTALBA

♈

½ *cup butter*
½ *cup thinly sliced white onion*
¼ *cup chopped shallots*
1 *tablespoon minced garlic*
½ *cup chopped mushrooms*
½ *cup chopped ham*
1 *cup diced potato, deep-fried light brown*
    and drained on absorbent paper
½ *cup white wine*
1 *tablespoon chopped parsley*
2 *pounds chicken leg, thigh and breast (boned)*
1½ *cups Bearnaise Sauce (page 185)*

In a 10-inch skillet melt butter and saute onion, shallots and garlic until tender. Add mushrooms, ham and potatoes and continue cooking about 5 minutes more. Add wine and parsley, heat through. Remove sauce from heat, keep warm. Dredge boned chicken pieces in seasoned flour and fry golden brown. To serve, arrange chicken pieces on bed of above sauce and cover chicken with Bearnaise Sauce. Flank with warm toast triangles and sprinkle lightly with paprika. 2 to 3 servings.

CHICKEN ROCHAMBEAU

♈

2 ready-to-cook chickens (2½ pounds each), disjointed
   and boned (use neck, skin and bones to make stock)
¾ cup butter
1 cup minced shallots
1 teaspoon minced garlic
2 tablespoons flour
2 cups chicken stock
½ cup chopped mushrooms
1 tablespoon Worcestershire sauce
½ teaspoon salt
Dash cayenne
½ cup Burgundy wine
4 Holland rusks
¼ pound sliced boiled ham
½ cup Bearnaise Sauce (page 185)

Dredge chicken in seasoned flour. Melt butter in large skillet and saute chicken until golden brown and tender. Remove to covered dish and keep warm. Saute shallots and garlic in drippings. Add flour and brown well. Stir in stock until smooth. Add mushrooms, simmer 15 minutes. Add Worcestershire sauce, salt, cayenne and burgundy. Heat through. Arrange Holland rusks on platter, cover with ham slices. Pour chicken sauce over ham. Arrange chicken pieces on sauce and cover chicken with Bearnaise Sauce. 4 servings.

CREPES CHANTICLEER

♔

CREPES

8 oz. flour
4 eggs
½ pt. milk

FILLING

4 oz. butter
1 cup flour
1 pt. chicken stock
½ cup finely minced chicken
½ cup finely minced mushrooms
1 tablespoon chopped parsley
1 teaspoon Worcestershire sauce
1 tablespoon sherry
Salt and cayenne pepper to taste

To make crepes, see Crepes Suzette. For filling, make a roux of butter and flour, melting butter and gradually blending in flour. Gradually blend in the chicken stock, then the sherry. Add chicken, mushrooms, parsley, and Worcestershire sauce. Season, and fill crepes, which are folded in half and placed back-to-back, two to a plate. Top filled crepes with more of the filling, and serve. Serves 6.

D I N D E   M U L L A D Y

♍

½ *cup butter*
2 *tablespoons flour*
2 *cups chicken stock*
⅓ *cup sauterne*
⅓ *cup seedless grapes (canned may be used)*
¼ *cup sliced water chestnuts*
Paprika
4 *Holland rusks*
4 *slices canned pineapple, grilled*
2 *pounds roast turkey breast*

In a skillet melt butter and stir in flour. Cook slowly stirring constantly, about 5 minutes, but do not brown. Blend in chicken stock until smooth. Simmer 10 to 12 minutes. Add wine, grapes and water chestnuts. Heat through. Remove from heat. Arrange rusk in bottom of shallow casserole. Next arrange pineapple slices on rusk and turkey slices on top. Cover with hot sauce and sprinkle with paprika. Bake at 350° (moderate oven) 20 to 25 minutes. 4 servings.

D U C K   C H E R R Y

♉

1 ready-to-cook Long Island duck (3 to 3½ pounds)
2 bay leaves
2 white onions
3 stalks celery
Salt and pepper
½ cup melted butter
3 tablespoons flour
2 cups chicken stock
½ cup dark sweet cherries
3 tablespoons cherry liqueur
3 tablespoons brandy

Wipe duck with damp cloth. Stuff with bay leaves, onion and celery. Salt and pepper duck and place in baking pan, brush with melted butter. Roast duck in preheated oven at 475° (very hot) for ½ to ¾ hour. Duck should not roast too dry. If no blood appears after being pierced with fork, duck is done. Remove from pan to warm serving platter and keep warm while making sauce. Stir flour into drippings and brown. Blend in chicken stock and bring to a boil. Remove from heat and strain into a saucepan. Add cherries to saucepan and simmer 3 to 5 minutes. Add cherry liqueur and brandy, heat through and pour over duck. 2 servings.

DUCK ORANGE

♥

1 ready-to-cook Long Island duck (3 to 3½ pounds)
2 bay leaves
2 white onions
3 stalks celery
Salt and pepper
½ cup melted butter
3 tablespoons flour
2 cups chicken stock
1 seedless orange peeled and sliced
3 tablespoons orange curacao or cointreau
3 tablespoons brandy

Wipe duck with damp cloth. Stuff with bay leaves, onion, celery. Salt and pepper duck and place in baking pan, brush with melted butter. Roast duck in preheated oven at 475° (very hot) for ½ to ¾ hour. Duck should not be roasted too dry. If no blood appears after being pierced with a fork, duck is done. Remove from pan to warm platter and keep warm while making sauce. Stir flour into drippings and brown. Blend in chicken stock and bring to a boil. Remove from heat and strain into a saucepan. Add orange slices and gently simmer 3 to 5 minutes. Add curacao and brandy, heat through and pour over duck. Garnish with thin half slices of seedless orange. 2 servings.

R O C K   C O R N I S H   H E N S

♉

½ *cup butter*
1 cup finely chopped onion
½ *cup finely chopped celery*
½ *cup finely chopped shallots*
½ *cup minced ham*
1½ *dozen oysters, chopped*
2 eggs slightly beaten
4 cups bread soaked in oyster water and squeezed dry
1 teaspoon powdered thyme
2 bay leaves
Salt and pepper to taste
2 tablespoons chopped parsley
2 Rock hens (boned)

In a 9-inch skillet melt butter and saute onion, celery, shallots and ham. Add oysters and heat through. Remove from heat, stir in eggs and bread. Mix thoroughly. Return the mixture to heat and add thyme, salt, pepper and parsley. Heat through. Stuff hens and tie legs together. Brush with melted butter, sprinkle with salt and pepper. Bake in preheated oven 350° (moderate) for 1 hour, or until done.

To make sauce: Remove roasted hens to serving platter and keep warm. Blend into the drippings 2 tablespoons flour and brown. Stir in 1½ cups chicken stock until smooth and cook until thickened. Strain and serve over hens. 2 servings.

Meat

BEEF TIPS A LA DEUTSCH

❦

⅛ cup butter
Salt and pepper
3 pounds sirloin beef tips, sliced
3 medium onions, sliced thin

In a large skillet melt butter. Salt and pepper beef tips and quickly sear slices on both sides. Reduce heat and saute 8 to 10 minutes. Add onions and saute together with beef for a few minutes more. 6 servings.

B E E F   D A U B E   G L A C E

❦

3 lbs. rump or round of veal, roasted well done
   (may be left-over)
2 quarts beef stock or consomme
3 tablespoons gelatin
2 tablespoons chopped pimientos
2 tablespoons chopped parsley
2 chopped dill pickles
Salt, pepper and cayenne

If you are using beef stock rather than consomme, it must be clarified. (Add 4 slightly beaten egg whites and 1 cut-up tomato to stock, bring slowly to a boil, simmer 5 minutes, and strain through a cloth.) Or use canned consomme. Dissolve gelatin in ½ cup cold water, and add to consomme. Boil quickly and remove to cool. Dice the meat, and put in a mold with parsley, pimientos, and pickle. Cover with clear consomme and chill overnight. This should be highly seasoned with salt, pepper and cayenne.

H A M   G L A C E

🍂

3 *lbs. diced ham (may be left-over)*
2 *cloves garlic*
1 *teaspoon thyme*
3–4 *cloves*
12 *peppercorns*
1 *tablespoon chopped parsley*
1 *tablespoon chopped pimientos*
3 *tablespoons gelatin*

Boil pieces of ham for 45 minutes with garlic, thyme, cloves, and peppercorns. Clarify stock as in Beef Daube Glace. Dissolve gelatin and add to stock. Pour over chopped ham, parsley and pimientos in mold, and chill overnight.

MARINATED FILET MIGNON

♘

4 filets mignon (14 ounces each)
6 truffles, sliced
2 slices bacon, quartered
Salt and pepper
1 teaspoon crushed black peppercorns
3 bay leaves
½ teaspoon allspice
3 to 6 cloves
1 cup brandy
1 cup Burgundy
1 cup vegetable oil
½ cup butter
3 tablespoons flour
2 cups beef stock
1 cup marinade
16 whole mushrooms

Make 2 slits in each filet about 3″ long and not quite to the under-side. Stuff these with slices of truffle, bacon pieces and salt and pepper. Make marinade in a 9x9x3″ pan or dish by combining the peppercorns, bay leaves, allspice, cloves, brandy, Burgundy and vegetable oil. Place prepared filets in this mixture and refrigerate for 24 hours or more. Remove and drain filets when ready to cook and grill according to taste, rare, medium or well done. To make sauce to cover melt the ½ cup butter in a small saucepan. Stir in flour and brown. Blend in until smooth the beef stock and the 1 cup of marinade. Stir in mushrooms and heat through. Pour sauce over filets. 4 servings.

FILET MIGNON STANLEY

2 filets (12 ounces each)
½ cup Bechamel Sauce (page 186)
⅓ cup horseradish
Pinch cayenne
4 bananas, peeled

Grill filets medium or rare. Combine next three ingredients for sauce. Dredge bananas in flour and saute in butter. Place filet in center of warm plate. Arrange a banana on either side of the filet and a heaping spoonful of sauce on alternate sides. Spoon meat juices over all and serve. 2 servings.

Meat

HAMBURGER BRENNAN

2 pounds ground beef
¼ cup minced shallots
¼ cup minced white onion
½ cup toasted Holland rusk crumbs
Dash nutmeg
1½ teaspoons salt
½ teaspoon pepper
2 tablespoons Worcestershire sauce
1 tablespoon chopped parsley
2 eggs

Combine all ingredients together thoroughly and shape into 6 patties (oval in shape) and grill.

SAUCE MAISON

¼ lb. butter
1 tablespoon Worcestershire sauce
¾ cup jus (from meat)
Pinch chopped parsley

Melt butter until golden brown. Add Worcestershire sauce and jus and cook 1 minute. Add parsley and serve with meat.

(148)

ROAST TENDERLOIN
or Filet of Beef Bordeaux

♉

1 filet of beef, 3½ pounds
Salt
Pepper
2 large cloves of garlic

Clean and wipe filet. Rub with salt and pepper. Crush garlic cloves and rub over meat. Place on rack in shallow baking pan and bake in preheated oven 375° ½ hour for rare, 45 minutes for medium, and 1 hour for well done. Slice and serve au jus. 6 servings.

SHISH KEBAB

♈

1 large bell pepper cut into 2-inch squares
4 large mushroom caps
½ large white onion, cut into 4 wedges
4 lamb chop eyes
1 teaspoon crushed black peppercorns
3 bay leaves
½ teaspoon allspice
3 to 6 cloves
1 cup brandy
1 cup Burgundy
1 cup vegetable oil

On 10″ skewer thread alternately bell pepper, mushroom, onion, and lamb. Combine remaining ingredients to make marinade. Marinate kabob for 24 hours or more in refrigerator. When ready to cook, drain kabob and grill 20 minutes on top of stove or broil under flame until meat reaches desired degree of doneness. 1 serving. Note: There is enough marinade to cover 6 such kabobs.

T O U R N E D O S   B R E N N A N

❦

2 tablespoons butter
½ cup sliced mushrooms
1 tablespoon flour
½ cup mushroom juice
¼ cup red wine
¼ teaspoon Worcestershire sauce
¼ teaspoon salt
Dash pepper
4 small filets mignon
1 large ripe tomato

In a small saucepan melt butter and saute mushrooms. Add flour and cook slowly a few minutes until slightly browned. Stir in wine, mushroom juice and seasonings. Cook until thickened. While this sauce is cooking, season and grill filet to taste (rare or medium rare). Cut the tomato into four nice slices and grill. Arrange tomato slice on each filet and pour mushroom sauce over all. 4 servings.

T O U R N E D O S   R O S S I N I

❦

¼ *cup butter*
1½ *tablespoons flour*
1 *cup beef stock*
⅓ *teaspoon (about 5) peppercorns, crushed*
1 *bay leaf*
1 *allspice*
1 *clove*
2 *tablespoons brandy*
2 *tablespoons Burgundy*
2 *tablespoons vegetable oil*
4 *filets mignon*
½ *pound pate of pork liver*
Truffles, sliced

In a small saucepan melt butter and stir in flour. Brown. Stir in beef stock until smooth. Add next seven ingredients and simmer 5 minutes. Remove bay leaf, allspice and clove. Grill filets to taste. To serve arrange a filet on a serving plate, arrange a large slice pate on top. Garnish top with slices of truffle. Pour hot sauce over all. 4 servings.

T O U R N E D O S   R O Y A L

♥

¼ *cup butter*
½ *cup chopped onion*
¼ *cup bread crumbs*
1 *teaspoon paprika*
1 *teaspoon capers*
1 *teaspoon chopped truffles*
Pinch powdered thyme
1 *cup sweetbreads, parboiled and chopped fine*
4 *artichoke cups*
¼ *cup Bearnaise Sauce (page 185)*
4 *filets mignon (12 to 14 ounces each)*

In a small skillet melt butter and saute onion, bread crumbs, paprika, capers, truffles and thyme until done. Add sweetbreads and heat through. Remove pan from heat. Divide mixture in 4 portions and roll into balls. Place each ball in an artichoke heart. While this is cooking, season filets and grill to taste. Place each filet on a serving plate. Pour about 1 tablespoon Bearnaise Sauce over filet and place stuffed artichoke heart on top. 4 servings.

VEAL GRILLADES AND GRITS*

6 veal steaks (4 oz. each)
2 large onions, coarsely chopped
4 green peppers coarsely chopped
½ cup coarsely chopped celery
4 finely chopped cloves of garlic
2 bay leaves
½ cup shortening
4–6 ripe tomatoes
1 qt. water or beef stock
2 tablespoons cornstarch
1 tablespoon lard
1 cup grits

Saute in shortening for 5–10 minutes celery, onions, green peppers, garlic and bay leaves. Add chopped tomatoes and beef stock and simmer for 20 minutes. Dissolve cornstarch in 3 tablespoons of water, and add gradually. Season with salt and pepper, and boil until it thickens. Remove from heat.

Season veal steaks and dip in flour. Saute until brown in 1 tablespoon of lard. Arrange in baking pan, cover with sauce and bake at 350° for ½ hour, or until veal is tender.

Cook grits according to instructions on package, and serve separately.

* This dish may also be served with rice.

R O U L A D E   O F   V E A L

🅜

½ cup butter
1 cup minced onion or shallots
½ cup minced celery
1½ dozen oysters, chopped
2 cups bread cubes, dampened with oyster water
1 egg, beaten
Pinch thyme
Salt and pepper to taste
1 teaspoon chopped parsley
4 veal cutlets
1 dill pickle, quartered
3 cups tomato sauce *

Melt butter in skillet and saute onion and celery until tender. Add oysters and stir while cooking 5 minutes more. Add bread cubes and heat through. Remove from heat and mix thoroughly with egg, thyme, salt and pepper. Add parsley. With edge of heavy saucer, pound cutlets thin. Fill centers with oyster dressing and ¼ dill pickle and roll. Secure with toothpicks. Sprinkle with salt and pepper and roll in flour. Place roulades in pan and bake in preheated oven 400° (moderately hot) 15 to 20 minutes, or until brown. Remove from oven. Cover with tomato sauce and simmer 20 minutes, or until done. Serve with Spanish Rice (page 168). 4 servings.

* See page 192 or use Heinz canned tomato sauce.

Game

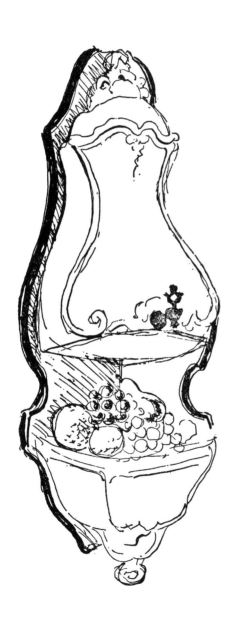

MARINATED VENISON

❧

MARINADE

1 tablespoon peppercorns, crushed
3 bay leaves
½ teaspoon allspice
3 to 6 cloves
1 cup brandy
1 cup Burgundy
1 cup vegetable oil

A haunch of venison
8 carrots, washed and scraped
8 small white onions, peeled

Mix together marinade ingredients and marinate venison for 24 hours or more. Venison will keep in this solution from 1 to 2 weeks if kept very well refrigerated.

Preheat oven to 375° F. Remove venison from marinade and drain. Place in shallow baking pan, arrange carrots and onions around meat. Dot meat with butter and drench with 1 cup marinade. Bake 15 minutes per pound. Baste every 10 minutes and turn meat occasionally to keep meat from drying out. When done remove meat and vegetables to serving dish and make a sauce with the drippings by adding ¼ cup butter, ¼ cup flour, 2 cups beef stock, 1 cup marinade and salt and pepper to taste. Simmer until thickened to gravy consistency.

PIGEON EN CASSEROLE

♉

2 *plump ready-to-cook pigeons*
⅓ *cup butter*
¼ *cup chopped green onion*
⅓ *cup chopped white onion*
½ *cup chopped celery*
3 *tablespoons flour*
2 *cups chicken stock*
½ *teaspoon salt*
Dash pepper
½ *cup red wine*
½ *cup small boiled carrots*
¼ *cup sliced boiled mushrooms*
¼ *cup boiled lima beans*

Split pigeons in half through center of breast. Open flat, brush with melted butter, salt and pepper and broil 20 to 25 minutes until brown. Place in a casserole and keep warm. In a skillet, melt the butter and saute the green onion, white onion and celery until tender. Stir in flour and brown. Blend in stock until smooth. Add salt and pepper, simmer 15 to 20 minutes. Add wine and simmer 5 minutes more. Pour carrots, mushrooms and lima beans over pigeon in casserole and cover with sauce. Bake at 350° (moderate oven) for 25 minutes. 2 servings.

PRESSED DUCK

🦆

1 wild duck, dressed and drawn
2 stalks celery
2 small onions, peeled
2 tablespoons melted butter
1 teaspoon butter
1 cup pressed stock (add chicken stock to make up volume,
    if necessary)
½ teaspoon Worcestershire sauce
1 teaspoon red currant jelly
5 black cherries
1 ounce brandy
1 ounce red wine

Fill duck cavity with celery stalks and whole onions. Brush duck
with the 2 tablespoons melted butter. Salt and pepper lightly.
Place in uncovered shallow pan and bake in preheated oven 450°
(hot) for 30 minutes, basting with hot water if necessary. Duck
should be nice and brown. Reduce heat to 425° and bake 15 minutes more. Remove duck from pan and carefully remove skin (in
one piece) working from center back slit. Roll and lift skin sever-
ing with sharp knife, first from one side and then the other. Meat of
breast and legs should be boned and rolled inside duck skin, breast
at top and meat of legs side by side just below. Keep warm. Place
remaining carcass of duck in press and get as much juice as possible. In a deep chafing dish, melt butter, pressed stock is next
added with Worcestershire sauce, jelly and cherries. Heat through.
Add duck to sauce and simmer a few minutes. Pour brandy and
wine over duck and carefully ignite. Baste until flame dies away.
Serve with remaining sauce poured over duck. 1 serving.

QUAIL IN WHITE WINE

2 ready-to-cook quail
½ cup butter
2 tablespoons flour
2 cups chicken stock
½ cup sauterne
Dash cayenne

Split quail down center breast and open flat. Brush lightly with melted butter and sprinkle with salt and pepper. Broil 15 to 20 minutes to golden brown. While quail is broiling, make sauce by melting butter in 4-quart saucepan. Stir in flour and cook, stirring, 5 to 7 minutes, being careful not to brown. Blend in stock and simmer 10 minutes. Add sauterne, salt and pepper. Add quail and simmer 15 to 20 minutes or until quail is done. 2 servings.

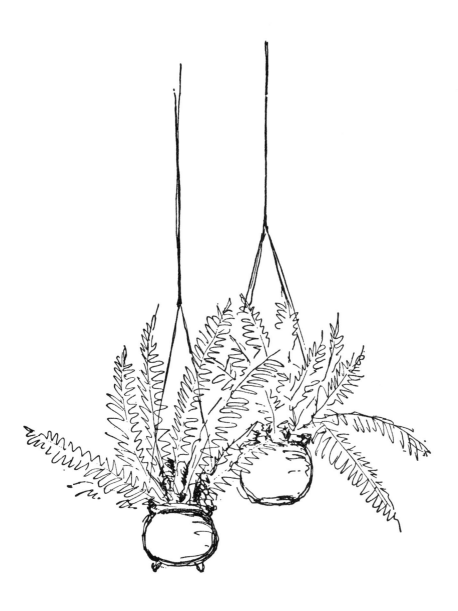

Rice Dishes

CREOLE JAMBALAYA

❧

½ cup chopped green onion
½ cup chopped white onion
⅓ cup chopped green pepper
½ cup chopped celery with a few leaves
1 teaspoon minced garlic
⅓ cup melted butter
½ pound raw shrimp, peeled and cleaned (about 1 cup)
2 dozen raw oysters (about 1 cup)
2 cups (16 oz.) whole tomatoes
1 cup water
Bay leaf
½ teaspoon salt
¼ teaspoon cayenne
1 cup raw rice, washed (unless otherwise directed
     on package)

In large saucepan saute onion, green pepper, celery and garlic in butter until tender. Add shrimp and oysters and cook five minutes more. Add remaining ingredients except rice and cook over low heat 10 to 15 minutes more. Add rice, stir and cover tightly; cook 25 to 30 minutes over low heat or until rice is done. 4 servings.

DUCK JAMBALAYA

♫

1 cup flour
1 teaspoon salt
¼ teaspoon cayenne
1 Long Island duck (3½ pounds, disjointed)
⅓ cup butter
1 cup finely chopped white onion
1 cup finely chopped green onion
4 cups chicken stock
2 cups raw rice

Combine flour with salt and cayenne, dredge duck in this mixture, retaining the leftover flour. In a Dutch oven with tight fitting lid, saute duck in butter until golden brown. Remove to platter and keep warm. Saute white and green onion in drippings until tender. Add remaining flour mixture to pan and brown well. Add chicken stock blending until smooth. Return duck to pan and simmer 20 minutes. Add rice, cover and cook over low heat 30 to 35 minutes. If rice has not absorbed all the sauce, continue cooking uncovered 8 to 10 minutes more. 3 to 4 servings.

R E D   B E A N S

♍

2 *cups red kidney beans*
½ *cup chopped white onion*
½ *cup chopped shallots*
½ *teaspoon minced garlic*
¼ *cup butter*
½ *cup chopped ham*
3 *cups water*
1 *teaspoon salt*
½ *teaspoon black pepper*

Soak beans in water to cover overnight. Drain. In a large saucepan saute onion, shallots, and garlic in butter until tender. Add ham and continue cooking until lightly browned. Add drained kidney beans and remaining ingredients. Cook slowly over low heat 45 minutes to 1 hour, adding more hot water if needed. Serve with hot, fluffy rice. 6 servings.

S P A N I S H R I C E

♉

½ *cup chopped green pepper*
¾ *cup chopped white onion*
⅓ *cup chopped ham*
½ *teaspoon Spanish saffron*
⅓ *cup butter*
3 cups cooked rice
½ *teaspoon white pepper*
⅓ *cup chopped pimiento*
1 tablespoon liquid from pimiento

In a 9-inch skillet over medium heat, saute green pepper, onion, ham and saffron in butter until tender. Stir in rice, pepper, pimiento and pimiento liquid, continue cooking until heated through. 4 to 6 servings.

WILD RICE

❦

½ *pound wild rice cooked according to package directions*
⅓ *cup chopped green onion*
½ *cup minced ham*
⅓ *cup butter*
¼ *cup chopped parsley*
Dash pepper

While rice is cooking, saute onion and ham in butter until ham is lightly browned. Add drained rice and continue cooking 5 minutes more. Remove skillet from heat. Stir in parsley and pepper. Serve immediately. 3 to 4 servings.

MUSHROOM RICE

❦

2 cups cooked rice
1 cup sliced mushrooms
½ *cup butter*
Salt and pepper

Saute mushrooms in butter. Add rice and saute for 10 minutes.

Vegetables

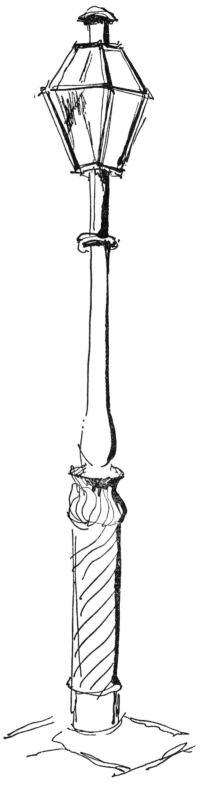

DĂUPHINE POTATOES

½ cup boiling water
⅓ cup butter, melted
Pinch salt
½ cup flour
1 egg
¾ teaspoon salt
¾ teaspoon nutmeg
1¾ cup cooked, mashed potatoes

In a saucepan over high heat boil water, then reduce heat to low and add butter, salt and flour, stirring constantly until mixture forms compact ball. Remove pan from heat and cool. Add egg, salt, nutmeg and beat until smooth. Add potatoes, mix thoroughly. Chill. Roll mixture into 1½″ balls and drop into fat heated to 375°. Fry until golden brown. 4 to 6 servings.

POTATOES SOUFFLÉ

♆

2 pounds Idaho or California potatoes
One deep fat fryer filled to frying level
and heated to 250°
One deep fat fryer filled to frying level
and heated to 400° or very hot

Peel and cut potatoes into lengthwise strips ⅛″ thick. Remove extra starch by washing under cold running water; drain and dry thoroughly. Put just enough potatoes into frying basket to cover bottom; never crowd potatoes together. Lower basket into fat heated to 250° and shake very gently while frying until potatoes rise to top of grease and begin to show slight signs of puffing on edges. (*If* potatoes *do not* show this slight puffing, they will not work, so discard them and start over.) When slight puffing begins transfer basket immediately to hot fat and cook until completely puffed and browned. Drain on absorbent paper, sprinkle with salt and serve while still warm. 6 servings.

STUFFED BAKED POTATOES

🎜

> 2 large Idaho potatoes, scrubbed
> 4 strips bacon, quartered
> ¼ cup chopped green onion
> 2 tablespoons grated Parmesan cheese
> ½ cup sour cream
> ½ teaspoon salt
> ½ teaspoon white pepper

Bake potatoes in hot oven 400° F. for 1 hour. While potato is cooling slightly to make handling easier, grill bacon pieces in 7-inch skillet until crisp. Drain off excess drippings leaving 3 tablespoons in skillet. Add onion and saute slowly. Remove skillet from heat. Cut shallow lengthwise slice from each potato and carefully spoon out inside; add to skillet. Add cheese, cream and seasonings, mixing and mashing to blend thoroughly. Return skillet to low heat and heat through. Stuff mixture into potatoes, drizzle with butter and dash paprika. Bake at 350° 15 to 20 minutes. 2 servings.

STUFFED TOMATOES

❧

6 large tomatoes
4 oz. butter
½ cup chopped green onions
2 cloves garlic
½ pound finely chopped ham *
1 cup wet squeezed bread
Salt, pepper, paprika and bread crumbs

Slice tops off tomatoes and scoop out. Chop meat of tomato. Saute onions in butter with garlic, chopped ham, and tomato. Add wet bread. Season with salt and pepper, stuff into tomato shells, cover with bread crumbs and paprika, dot with butter and bake at 350° for 10 minutes. Serves 6.

* Shrimp or crab meat may be used.

STUFFED BELL PEPPERS

♥

6 green peppers
½ cup butter
½ cup chopped green onions
½ cup chopped onions
2 cloves chopped garlic
½ lb. ground meat
1 cup wet squeezed bread
3 eggs
Salt, pepper, bread crumbs

Cut off tops of peppers, remove insides and boil 5 minutes. Saute onions in butter, add ground meat and chopped garlic and cook 5 or 10 minutes. Add bread, work in eggs, season and cook 5 more minutes. Stuff peppers, sprinkle with bread crumbs, dot with butter and bake 5 minutes at 350°. Serves 6.

STUFFED EGGPLANT

❦

3 eggplants
1 cup chopped green onions
½ cup chopped onions
2 cloves garlic
1 tablespoon thyme
2 bay leaves
½ cup butter
2 cups wet squeezed bread
2 lbs. cooked, chopped shrimp *
3 eggs
Bread crumbs
Salt, pepper, paprika, parsley

Parboil eggplants in skins, split in half, for 10 minutes. Let cool, scoop out of shells, and chop. Saute onions in butter with finely chopped garlic, thyme, and bay leaves for 5 minutes, without browning. Add 2 cups of wet bread, shrimp and eggplant. Mix together and gradually add eggs. Season with salt, pepper, and parsley. Cook for 5 minutes, stirring constantly. Remove from fire and stuff into eggplant shells. Sprinkle with bread crumbs and paprika, dot with butter, and bake for 5 or 10 minutes at 350°. Serves 6.

* Ham or crab meat may be used instead.

STUFFED MIRLETONS
(Vegetable Pears)

6 mirletons
½ cup butter
½ cup chopped onions
½ cup chopped green onions
2 cloves chopped garlic
1 lb. crab meat
1 cup squeezed wet bread
2 eggs
Salt, pepper, and bread crumbs

Boil whole mirletons for twenty minutes. Split in half, remove seeds and scoop out meat. Proceed as in Stuffed Eggplant and Stuffed Tomato. Serves 6.

STUFFED SQUASH

🌱

6 *young squash*
½ *cup chopped green onions*
½ *cup chopped onions*
3 *cloves chopped garlic*
½ *cup butter*
1 *cup chopped ham*
1 *cup squeezed wet bread*
3 *eggs*
Salt, pepper and bread crumbs

Boil squash for 10 minutes. Cut in half and scoop out. Proceed as in Stuffed Eggplant and Stuffed Tomato.

YAMS RICHARD

❦

3 pounds yams
¼ teaspoon nutmeg
¼ teaspoon cinnamon
¼ cup butter, melted
½ cup light cream
⅓ cup chopped pecans
⅓ cup seedless raisins
16 marshmallows

Boil yams until tender. Peel and mash; then add next 6 ingredients mixing thoroughly. Place in a buttered 2-quart casserole. Cover top with marshmallows. Bake in 350° F. oven 25 to 30 minutes. 6 servings.

Sauces

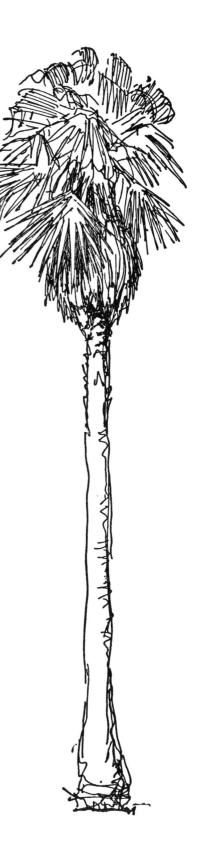

BEARNAISE SAUCE

🍷

4 egg yolks
Juice of 1 lemon
2 cups melted butter
Salt and pepper
2 tablespoons capers
¼ cup chopped parsley
1 tablespoon tarragon vinegar

In top half of boiler, beat egg yolks and lemon juice. Cook slowly in double boiler over very low heat, never allowing water in bottom pan to come to a boil. Slowly add melted butter to above mixture, stirring constantly with a wooden spoon. Add salt, pepper (to taste), capers, parsley and vinegar. Stir to blend. 2 cups.

BECHAMEL SAUCE

❦

½ cup butter
½ cup flour
1 cup chicken stock
1 cup light cream
1 teaspoon salt
½ teaspoon cayenne

In a heavy saucepan melt butter and stir in flour. Stir constantly while cooking 8 to 10 minutes on very low heat. Do not brown. Gradually stir in stock and then cream to smooth blend. Add salt and cayenne. Continue cooking to sauce consistency. 2½ cups.

BORDELAISE SAUCE

❧

½ *cup olive oil*
1 tablespoon minced garlic
1 tablespoon minced parsley

Combine ingredients and chill. ½ cup.

HEMENWAY SAUCE

❧

1 tablespoon anchovy paste
1 lemon
¼ *lb. butter*

Put the butter in a saucepan with the anchovy paste and the juice of 1 lemon. Stir until melted and blended together. Serve with meat. 4 servings.

CREAM SAUCE

¾ *cup butter*
1 cup flour
3 cups milk
1½ teaspoons salt
½ teaspoon cayenne

In a heavy saucepan melt butter and stir in flour. Stir constantly while cooking 8 to 10 minutes on very low heat. Do not brown. Gradually stir in milk to a smooth mixture. Add salt and cayenne. Continue cooking to sauce consistency. 3½ to 4 cups.

FISH BECHAMEL SAUCE

¾ cup butter
1 cup finely chopped green onion
1 cup flour
2½ cups fish stock
¾ cup white wine
1 teaspoon salt
½ teaspoon cayenne
2 egg yolks, beaten

In a 9-inch skillet melt butter over medium heat. Saute green onions until tender, about five minutes. Blend in the flour thoroughly, cook slowly about five minutes more, stirring constantly; do not brown flour. Remove skillet from heat. Blend in fish stock, wine, salt and pepper until smooth. Blend in egg yolks. Return pan to heat and gently cook over low heat stirring constantly about 15 minutes more. Sauce will be thick. Yield: 4 cups.

HOLLANDAISE SAUCE

♎

4 egg yolks
2 tablespoons lemon juice
½ pound butter, melted
¼ teaspoon salt

In top half of double boiler, beat egg yolks and stir in lemon juice. Cook very slowly in double boiler over low heat, never allowing water in bottom pan to come to a boil. Add butter a little at a time, stirring constantly with a wooden spoon. Add salt and pepper. Continue cooking slowly until thickened. 1 cup.

MARCHAND DE VIN SAUCE

¾ cup butter
⅓ cup finely chopped mushrooms
½ cup minced ham
⅛ cup finely chopped shallots
½ cup finely chopped onion
2 tablespoons garlic, minced
2 tablespoons flour
½ teaspoon salt
⅛ teaspoon pepper
Dash cayenne
¾ cup beef stock
½ cup red wine

In a 9-inch skillet melt butter and lightly saute the mushrooms, ham, shallots, onion and garlic. When the onion is golden brown, add the flour, salt, pepper and cayenne. Brown well, about 7 to 10 minutes. Blend in the stock and the wine and simmer over low heat for 35 to 45 minutes. Yield: 2 cups.

TOMATO SAUCE

½ *stalk celery*
1 *large onion coarsely sliced*
4 *carrots coarsely sliced*
2 *or 3 pods garlic*
3 *tablespoons lard*
1½ *tablespoons paprika*
2 *tablespoons flour*
2 *cans tomatoes*
1 *pint beef stock*

Saute carrots, onions, celery and garlic in lard. Add paprika, and mix flour in well. Add tomatoes and beef stock. Season with salt and pepper and simmer 20–25 minutes. Strain through fine sieve. Reheat for 5 minutes.

Salads

BLACKSTONE SALAD

❦

Pineapple ring
Orange sections
Grapefruit sections
Apple sections
Strips of bell pepper
Strips of pimiento

On a bed of lettuce lay pineapple ring, split in half and divided slightly (to make a larger space). Fill in with alternating orange, grapefruit and apple sections. Garnish with strips of pimiento and pepper and top with a dark cherry. For a dressing you may use either whipped cream with pineapple juice added, or honey thinned with lemon juice.

C A E S A R   S A L A D

🍷

Romaine lettuce
1 raw egg dipped in boiling water
1 pod garlic
½ lemon
2 strips anchovy
½ teaspoon horse radish
2 tablespoons wine vinegar
1½ tablespoons salad oil
1 teaspoon Parmesan cheese
Worcestershire sauce
Croutons

Break Romaine in salad bowl. Mix all the rest of the ingredients together and add.

CRAYFISH SALAD

♥

⅓ cup finely chopped celery
¼ cup minced parsley
2 tablespoons finely chopped pimiento
½ teaspoon white pepper
¼ teaspoon salt
¼ cup mayonnaise
4 cups boiled and peeled crayfish
Crisp salad greens

Mix first 6 ingredients together thoroughly. Add crayfish and mix well; chill. Mold in mounds and serve bed of greens. Garnish with slices of cucumber and radish roses. Sprinkle lightly with paprika. 4 servings.

OYSTER SALAD

⚱

⅓ *cup finely chopped celery*
¼ *cup minced parsley*
2 *tablespoons finely chopped pimiento*
¼ *teaspoon white pepper*
¼ *teaspoon salt*
⅓ *cup thick French dressing* *
4 *cups chopped poached* † *oysters*

Thoroughly mix first six ingredients; chill. Poach oysters in boiling water. Drain, chop and chill. Add oysters to dressing and mix lightly. Serve in mounds on bed of greens. Garnish with tomato slices or wedges. 4 servings.

* Thicken French dressing by beating it.
† Poaching differs from boiling in that very little water is used, barely to cover. You may add wine vinegar or lemon juice.

SCALLOP SALAD

❦

⅛ cup thick French dressing
⅛ cup finely chopped celery
¼ cup minced parsley
2 tablespoons finely chopped pimiento
¼ teaspoon white pepper
¼ teaspoon salt
3 cups cooked scallops, chilled *
Crisp salad greens

Thoroughly mix first six ingredients; chill. Arrange ¾ cup scallops on bed of crisp salad greens for each serving. Cover with above dressing and garnish with tomato wedges and parsley. 4 servings

* Boil 8–10 minutes.

WILLIAM SALAD

♉

⅓ *cup crab meat*
1 doz. boiled shrimp

DRESSING

1 hard boiled egg, mashed
2 anchovies, mashed
2 crisp slices bacon, mashed
Garlic
Oil and vinegar to taste

Mix all ingredients together and place on leaves of lettuce. 1 serving.

SEAFOOD SALAD JAMES

♌

1 doz. boiled shrimp
⅓ cup crab meat
1 tomato, quartered
2 asparagus
Chopped celery, escarolle, endive and lettuce

DRESSING

Vinegar, oil, hot sauce, catsup
Worcestershire sauce, white pepper and salt

Into dressing mix well shrimp, crab meat and chopped ingredients. Place mixture on Romaine and garnish with quartered tomato and asparagus.

CHICKEN SALAD THEODORE

⚓

⅛ *cup chicken, cubed*
Chopped celery and parsley
Slivers of almonds
1 hard boiled egg, quartered
2 radishes
Mayonnaise dressing

Mix cubed chicken and chopped ingredients with mayonnaise dressing. Place mixture on lettuce leaves. Garnish with quartered hard boiled egg and sprinkle with slivers of toasted almonds.

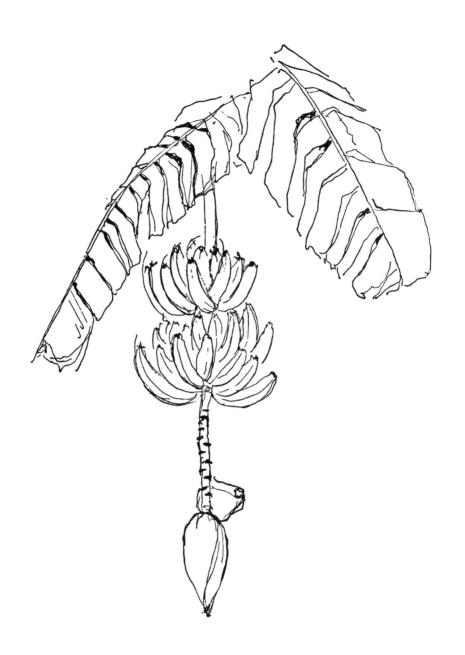

*D*esserts

BABA BRULOT

✹

1 baba au rum
2 oz. white rum
1 large scoop vanilla custard ice cream

Heat flat chafing dish over flame, then place in center of dish the cake and rum. Using a spoon with long handle, constantly baste cake with warm rum until cake is heated through. Ignite and when flame burns off serve cake over ice cream with remaining warm sauce. 1 serving.

BANANAS FOSTER

❧

2 tablespoons brown sugar
1 tablespoon butter
1 ripe banana, peeled and sliced lengthwise
Dash cinnamon
½ oz. banana liqueur
1 oz. white rum
1 large scoop vanilla cream

Melt brown sugar and butter in flat chafing dish. Add banana and saute until tender. Sprinkle with cinnamon. Pour in banana liqueur and rum over all and flame. Baste with warm liquid until flame burns out. Serve immediately over ice cream. 1 serving.

CARAMEL CUP CUSTARD

♉

6 egg yolks
1 cup sugar
¼ teaspoon salt
2 cups milk
½ teaspoon vanilla
Dash nutmeg

Beat together egg yolks, ½ cup sugar, salt and nutmeg to mix. Scald milk and pour into egg mixture. Stir to blend. Stir in vanilla.

In a small iron skillet, caramelize the other ½ cup sugar. Pour a little into each of 6 custard cups. When caramel sets, pour custard mixture into cups. Set cups in pan of hot water 1 inch deep. Bake in preheated oven 350° (moderate) 45 to 50 minutes or until silver knife inserted 1 inch from edge comes out clean. Quickly remove from heat and allow to cool. Unmold and serve. 6 servings.

BREAD PUDDING
WITH WHISKEY SAUCE

♗

10 slices day old bread, broken in pieces
4 cups milk, scalded
1 cup cream
4 eggs
1 cup sugar
1 teaspoon vanilla
1 teaspoon cinnamon
½ teaspoon nutmeg
¼ cup butter, melted
½ cup seedless raisins

Combine bread, milk and cream. Beat eggs; add sugar and mix well. Stir in bread mixture and add vanilla, cinnamon and nutmeg. Stir in butter and raisins. Pour into buttered 2 quart baking dish, set in a pan of warm water about 1 inch deep. Bake in 350° oven for 1 hour or until knife inserted in center comes out clean. 8 servings.

WHISKEY SAUCE

3 egg yolks
1 cup sugar
1 teaspoon vanilla
1½ cups milk
1 tablespoon cornstarch
¼ cup water
1½ ounces brandy

In a saucepan slightly beat egg yolks then add the next three ingredients and blend well. Cook over low heat until mixture comes to a boil. Blend cornstarch in water and stir into hot mixture. Continue cooking until thickened. Remove from heat and stir in brandy. Serve when cooled.

CREPES 417

♘

2 crepes *
2 pats butter
1 teaspoon white sugar
Peel of ½ lemon
Peel of 1 orange
Juice of ½ lemon
Juice of 1 orange
Chopped fruit and nuts in rum
¼ oz. Grand Marnier
¼ oz. Cherry Heering

Fill crepes with chopped fruit and nuts soaked in rum. In a sauce-pan put the butter, sugar, lemon and orange, and simmer until it thickens. Add Grand Marnier and Cherry Heering. Flame and pour over filled crepes. Serves 1.

* See recipe for Crepes Suzette, page 212.

CREPES FITZGERALD

♈

2 crepes *
2 heaping teaspoons Philadelphia Cream Cheese
2 tablespoons sour cream
½ cup strawberries
Sugar
Butter
Strawberry liqueur
Kirsch

Roll cream cheese and sour cream in crepes and put on plate. In a chafing dish, cook strawberries in sugar and butter. Flame in strawberry liqueur and Kirsch and pour over crepes. 1 serving.

* See recipe for Crepes Suzette, page 212.

CREPES SUZETTE

❦

¾ *cup sifted flour*
Pinch of salt
1 teaspoon sugar
2 eggs
Milk

Mix eggs with flour, sugar and salt. Add milk until batter is consistency of condensed milk. Beat until smooth. Heat a 6-inch skillet oiled with pastry brush dipped in vegetable oil. Pour batter (2 tablespoons) into pan, tilting quickly to distribute batter evenly. Cook 1 minute or so, until brown then turn and brown other side. Oil pan with brush, and repeat. Keep cooked cakes warm in a towel.

¼ *cup butter*
¼ *cup sugar*
Peel of 3 oranges, thinly slivered
Peel of 1 lemon, thinly slivered
Juice of 1 orange
Juice of ½ lemon
¾ *oz. cointreau*
¾ *oz. Grand Marnier*
2 oz. brandy

In a flat heated chafing dish, melt butter. Add sugar, mix well. Add peels and juice of lemons and oranges. Simmer until transparent. Place cakes 3 at a time in this sauce and fold in halves and quarters. Repeat until 12 cakes are in chafing dish. Pour the Cointreau, the Grand Marnier and then the brandy evenly over the cakes. Tip chafing dish slightly so that flame will ignite brandy. Level pan and move in a light forward and backward motion until flame on cakes dies down. Serve 3 cakes per person spooning some of the remaining sauce over the cakes. 4 servings.

E C L A I R   E U G E N E

❦

½ ounce white creme de menthe
1 ounce brandy
½ ounce bitter chocolate
1 teaspoon vanilla
1 tablespoon heavy cream
2 heaping tablespoons confectioners' sugar
1 pastry shell
2 scoops vanilla ice cream

Place a deep chafing dish over flame and warm the creme de menthe and brandy. Add the next four ingredients. When chocolate is nearly melted, ignite the mixture in the chafing dish and stir constantly while flaming to blend. Just as flame dies, spoon sauce over eclair filled with ice cream. Serve immediately. 1 serving.

O M E L E T   A U   R U M

♃

2 *eggs*
1 *tablespoon milk or cream*
¼ *teaspoon salt*
1 *tablespoon butter*
2 *tablespoons apple jelly*
1 *oz. light rum*

Make an omelet according to recipe on page 50. Fold 1 tablespoon of the apple jelly inside the omelet and place the other tablespoon of jelly beside it on hot serving plate. Pour the rum over the omelet, and flame.

OMELET AU STRAWBERRIES

❦

½ *cup fresh strawberries*
2 *tablespoons sugar*
2 *eggs*
1 *tablespoon milk or cream*
¼ *teaspoon salt*
1 *tablespoon butter*

Wash and drain strawberries. Heat berries and sugar in skillet. Crush lightly with spoon. Make an omelet according to recipe on page 50 and fold 1 tablespoon of the strawberries inside. Pour remaining strawberries over omelet. 1 serving.

PEACHES FLAMBÉE

2 large canned peach halves
2 tablespoons flour
½ cup butter
2 thin slivers of orange peel
2 thin slivers of lemon peel
2 oz. brandy

Dredge peach halves in flour. Saute in butter in small skillet or omit butter and deep fry in hot oil (375°) until golden brown. Place peach halves, cut side down, on warm platter. Garnish with orange and lemon peel. Pour brandy over peaches and ignite, basting until flame burns off. Serve with remaining warm brandy. 1 serving.

PRALINE PARFAIT SAUCE

2 cups dark cane syrup
⅓ cup sugar
⅓ cup boiling water
1 cup chopped pecans (or small halves)

Combine all ingredients in a saucepan and bring to boil over medium heat. As soon as mixture reaches a boiling stage, remove from heat immediately. Cool and store in a covered jar.

To make a Praline Parfait spoon alternate layers of vanilla ice cream and Praline Parfait Sauce into a tall parfait glass, ending with a layer of sauce. Top with whipped cream. Garnish with pecan halves.

STRAWBERRY FLAME

♈

Slice of pound cake
Strawberries
Sugar
Meringue
Absinthe (optional)
Brandy

Cover a slice of pound cake with strawberries that have been marinated in sugar and water. Build up over strawberries a peak of meringue, sweetened to taste and flavored with absinthe (optional). Put under broiler to brown. In peak of meringue set a half egg shell filled with brandy. Light brandy as dessert is brought to table. 1 serving.

SUGAR SHELL SHEBA

♉

1 meringue shell
1 scoop vanilla ice cream
Whipped cream
Chopped nuts
Sliced apricots
Apricot liqueur

Fill a shallow meringue shell with ice cream and top with whipped cream and nuts. Heat apricots in chafing dish pan, and flame them in apricot liqueur. Pour over ice cream filled meringue shell.

Specialties

CAFÉ BRULOT

✲

1 cinnamon stick, 4"
12 whole cloves
Peel of 2 oranges, cut in thin slivers
Peel of 2 lemons, cut in thin slivers
6 sugar lumps
8 ounces brandy
2 ounces curacao
1 quart strong, black coffee

In a brulot bowl or chafing dish, mash cinnamon, cloves, orange peel, lemon peel and sugar lumps with ladle. Add brandy and curacao, stir together. Carefully ignite brandy and mix until sugar is dissolved. Gradually add black coffee and continue mixing until flame flickers out. Serve hot in brulot cups or demi tasse. 10 to 12 servings.

ORANGE BRULOT

*1 thin skin orange, washed and dried and
plunged into hot water for 5 minutes*
1½ ounces cognac
1 lump sugar

With a sharp pointed knife, cut through peel only of the center of the orange. Insert the edge of a thin spoon between the skin and pulp working around entire orange, thus separating them. Carefully roll the skin up from the pulp, turning it inside out; upper half making a cup, lower half making a stand for the orange. Fill the "cup" with the cognac. Put lump sugar in a teaspoon filled with cognac and ignite. When sugar begins to color, gently float onto surface of cognac in orange cup. When flame flickers, blow out. 1 serving.

GARLIC BREAD

1 loaf French bread
4 cloves garlic, peeled
½ cup butter, melted
¼ cup grated Parmesan cheese
1 tablespoon minced parsley
1 teaspoon paprika

Thoroughly rub outside crust of bread with 2 slightly crushed cloves of garlic. Split loaf in half lengthwise. Completely cover cut surface with melted butter. Combine cheese, parsley and paprika and sprinkle over buttered surface. Press remaining 2 cloves garlic in garlic press over all. Put in oven at 350° about 5–10 minutes or until very hot. 6 servings.

Drinks

ABSINTHE FRAPPE

❦

1 ounce absinthe
2 dashes anisette or simple syrup

Fill an 8 ounce highball glass with shaved ice and add the above ingredients. Then add water or soda slowly, agitating ice and liquid until frost appears on outside of glass.

ABSINTHE SUISSESSE

❦

1¼ ounces absinthe
1 egg white
1 ounce cream
½ ounce orgeat syrup
4 ounces shaved ice

Rotate for about 5 seconds in a Waring blender and pour into a chilled Old Fashioned glass.

AMBROSIA

♉

⅓ ounce lemon juice
½ ounce cointreau
1 ounce brandy
Champagne

Shake and strain lemon juice, cointreau and brandy into chilled saucer champagne glass. Add champagne to fill glass.

CHABLIS CASSIS

♉

4 ounces Chablis
½ teaspoon creme de cassis
Twist of lemon peel

Pour 4 ounces of cold Chablis in a 5 ounce saucer champagne glass. Add creme de cassis. Stir gently and add twist of lemon peel.

NEW ORLEANS GIN FIZZ
or
Ramos Gin Fizz

❦

1 ounce lemon juice
2 teaspoons superfine granulated sugar
1 egg white
1 dash vanilla
2 dashes orange flower water
2 ounces breakfast cream or milk
1 ounce gin

Shake together thoroughly and strain into an 8 ounce highball glass.

HALF AND HALF

❦

1½ ounces dry vermouth
1½ ounces sweet vermouth

Put into an Old Fashioned glass with 2 ice cubes, stir gently, and serve with a twist of lemon peel.

MILK PUNCH

❦

1¼ *ounces bourbon or brandy*
3 *ounces breakfast cream or milk*
1 *teaspoon superfine powdered sugar*
1 *dash vanilla*

Shake thoroughly and strain into 8 ounce highball glass, and top with nutmeg.

MINT JULEP

❦

2 *ounces bourbon whiskey*
4 *sprigs fresh mint*
½ *ounce simple syrup*

Put these ingredients into a tall 14 ounce glass or silver mug. Fill with shaved ice and agitate with a mixing spoon until the outside of the glass or mug is coated with frost. Garnish with a generous bouquet of mint, a slice of orange, and a cherry. Serve with short straws (so that bouquet of mint will be appreciated while sipping).

OJEN COCKTAIL

❦

3 dashes Peychaud Bitters
1½ ounces Ojen

Shake thoroughly and strain into 3-ounce chilled cocktail glass.

PIRATE'S DREAM

❦

½ oz. grenadine
1 oz. Bacardi Rum
1 oz. Myer's Rum
1 oz. Christopher Columbus Rum
1 oz. Ronrico 151 Proof Rum
2 dashes Angostura Bitters
Juice of 1 orange
Juice of 1 lemon
8–10 cherries
Fresh green mint

In a large glass capable of holding 26–28 ounces, crush a couple of sprigs of mint. Add rum, grenadine, orange and lemon juice and bitters. Make sure that the mint is well blended into the other ingredients. Fill the glass with crushed ice, adding cherries throughout so that they will be spaced through the drink. As a last touch add cherries to the top of the drink, and a slice of orange and a slice of lemon to decorate the rim. Serve with 8 or 10 straws.

SAZERAC COCKTAIL

♥

2 *dashes simple syrup*
1 *dash Angostura Bitters*
2 *dashes Peychaud Bitters*
1¼ *ounces bourbon or rye whiskey*

Stir the above ingredients together in a mixing glass. Put 3 dashes of absinthe into a chilled Old Fashioned glass. Roll around to coat inside of glass and discard. Then strain drink from mixing glass into Old Fashioned glass and add a twist of lemon peel. This drink should not be served with ice.

New Recipes

COLD REDFISH BAYOU

♊

4-pound Redfish
2 bay leaves
Sprig of thyme
Piece of celery
1 medium-size onion, halved
1 lemon, cut in half
1 can chopped pimentos
1 bunch shallots, chopped
2 tablespoons chopped parsley
Salt and pepper
2 tablespoons unflavored gelatine
Sliced fresh tomatoes
Hardboiled eggs
Remoulade Sauce (page 71)

Put the Redfish in a pot and cover with cold water. Add bay leaves, thyme, celery and onion. Squeeze the lemon, then drop in the halves, rind and all. Boil for 20 minutes. Take off fire and allow to cool. Remove the fish from the stock and pick all the fish off the bones.

Place the picked fish in a dish, add the pimentos, shallots, parsley, salt and pepper to taste. Mix ingredients well into the fish.

Return the fish stock to the fire, adding gelatine that has been softened in cold water. Reboil stock, take off fire, and strain carefully through a cloth. Place fish in a mold, barely cover with stock, and chill for 2 or 3 hours.

Unmold on a platter. Garnish with sliced tomatoes and hardboiled eggs, and top with Remoulade Sauce. Serves 6.

CREPES FRUIT DE MER

❧

> 4 large (18″) pancakes
> ½ pound butter
> ½ cup flour
> 2 teaspoons paprika
> ½ quart milk
> 2 ounces sherry
> Salt and pepper
> 1 pound boiled scallops
> 2 pounds shrimp, boiled and peeled
> Hollandaise Sauce (page 190)

Make large crepes (medium-thin pancakes) using an 18″ frying pan. An extra light pancake mix may be used (or see page 212).

Melt butter, add flour and paprika, blending over a low heat. Add milk, stirring constantly until thickened. Add sherry, salt and pepper to taste, and finally add the shrimp and scallops.

Place each crepe flat on plate, put 3 tablespoons of the seafood mixture in the middle and then fold each end over. Crepes should then be placed with the folds on the bottom. Top with Hollandaise Sauce. Serves 4.

EGGS NOUVELLE ORLEANS

❦

½ *cup melted butter*
1 *pound fresh crabmeat*
8 *eggs*
1½ *cups Cream Sauce (page 188)*
     with 1 ounce brandy added
Salt and pepper

Melt butter in a skillet and add crabmeat and salt and pepper to taste. Sauté the crabmeat for about 6 minutes over medium heat.

Poach the eggs (in a pot of water with 1 cup of vinegar added).

Divide the sautéed crabmeat among 4 ramekins and cover each portion with 2 poached eggs. Top with brandy cream sauce. Serve immediately with toast or garlic bread. Serves 4.

EGGS ROYAL

❧

1 pound chicken livers, chopped fine
⅓ cup shallots, chopped very fine
3 egg yolks
8 eggs
1 cup Demi-Hollandaise Sauce

Mix the chicken livers, shallots and egg yolks. Place in a mold, then in a pan of water, and bake at 375° for about 25 to 30 minutes. After baking, remove from mold and slice like bread.

In each of 4 ramekins place 2 slices of the paté, and cover with two raw eggs. Bake in 350° oven for about 4 minutes, depending on how soft you like your eggs. Remove from oven and top with Demi-Hollandaise. Demi-Hollandaise is made by combining Cream Sauce (page 188) with Hollandaise Sauce (page 190), and after both are well blended, adding 1 ounce of brandy.

Must be served immediately. Serves 4.

GAZPACHO SOUP

❦

2 medium-size cucumbers
1 bunch shallots
2 whole tomatoes
1 medium-size green pepper
2 cloves garlic
1 teaspoon chopped parsley
2 small cans tomato juice
2 cups beef bouillon
1 tablespoon vinegar
2 teaspoons Worcestershire sauce
½ teaspoon Tabasco

Finely chop and combine cucumbers, shallots, tomatoes, green pepper, garlic and parsley. Put in a bowl and add tomato juice, bouillon, vinegar, Worcestershire sauce and Tabasco. Chill and serve. Serves 4.

OYSTERS HOLIDAY

❦

1 pound diced bacon
1 cup strained Turtle Soup (page 87)
½ cup finely chopped parsley
1 #3 can pimentos
2 tablespoons garlic, chopped fine
3 bunches shallots
3 green peppers
Tabasco sauce
Worcestershire sauce
Salt and pepper
3 dozen large oysters

Fry the bacon, but do not drain. Add garlic, shallots and green peppers to the bacon, and cook for a few minutes. Add Turtle Soup, parsley and pimentos, and season with Tabasco, pepper, salt and Worcestershire sauce.

Bake the oysters, 6 to a serving, on a base of rock salt, until the edges begin to curl.

Remove platters of oysters from the oven, cover each oyster with the sauce, and serve immediately. Serves 6.

OYSTERS AINSWORTH

❦

1 pound chicken livers, chopped fine
3 egg yolks
⅓ cup shallots, chopped fine
Crumbs of 6 Holland rusks
Salt and pepper
1 dozen fried oysters
Bearnaise Sauce (page 185)

Mix all ingredients with the exception of the oysters and sauce. Place in a mold, then in a pan of water, and bake at 375° for 25 to 30 minutes.

Remove paté from mold and slice like bread. Place each slice on a slice of toast. Top with three oysters (4, if small), and cover with Bearnaise. Serves 4.

PIGEONNEAUX ACADIAN

2 tablespoons butter
½ pound chicken livers
½ pound chicken gizzards
¼ pound ham, chopped fine
1 bunch green onions, chopped
2 cups French bread, soaked in stock or
    water, and squeezed dry
¼ bunch chopped parsley
4 squabs

Sauté in butter the chicken livers, gizzards, ham and green onion. Season to taste, add the bread, and stir constantly on low heat for about 10 minutes. Add the chopped parsley.

Roast squabs at 450° for thirty minutes. Let cool, then stuff squabs, tie the legs and return to oven at 450° for 20 minutes more. Serves 4.